Whole Body Reset
Cookbook for Beginners

1500 Days Simple Recipes and 4 Weeks Meal Plan to Boost Your Metabolism,
for a Flat Belly and Optimum Health at Midlife and Beyond

Nancy Ginsberg

© Copyright 2022 – All rights reserved.

The content contained within this book may not be reproduced, duplicated or transmitted without direct written permission from the author or the publisher.

Under no circumstances will any blame or legal responsibility be held against the publisher, or author, for any damages, reparation, or monetary loss due to the information contained within this book, either directly or indirectly.

Legal Notice:

This book is copyright protected. It is only for personal use. You cannot amend, distribute, sell, use, quote or paraphrase any part, or the content within this book, without the consent of the author or publisher.

Disclaimer Notice:

Please note the information contained within this document is for educational and entertainment purposes only. All effort has been executed to present accurate, up to date, reliable, complete information. No warranties of any kind are declared or implied. Readers acknowledge that the author is not engaged in the rendering of legal, financial, medical or professional advice. The content within this book has been derived from various sources. Please consult a licensed professional before attempting any techniques outlined in this book.

By reading this document, the reader agrees that under no circumstances is the author responsible for any losses, direct or indirect, that are incurred as a result of the use of the information contained within this document, including, but not limited to, errors, omissions, or inaccuracies.

Table of Content

Introduction 7

Fundamentals of Whole Body Reset 8
    What is the Whole Body Reset? 8
    The Advantages of Whole Body Reset 10
    Guidelines of Whole Body Reset 11
    Dietary Tips for the Whole Body Reset 13
    FAQS 14

4-Week Diet Plan 15
    Week 1 15
    Week 2 16
    Week 3 17
    Week 4 18

Chapter 1 Breakfast and Smoothie Recipes 19
    Spinach-Pear Smoothie 19
    Slow-Cooked Granola 19
    Carrot-Peach Soup with Nuts 20
    Banana-Yam Smoothie 20
    Sweet and Sour Raspberry Smoothie 21
    Citrusy Berry Smoothie 21
    Refreshing Papaya Smoothie 21
    Grain, Nuts, and Fruit Cereal 22
    Morning Oatmeal 22
    Sweet Potatoes and Cheese Ole 23
    Mexican Ranch-style Eggs 23
    Spanish Sausage Tortilla 24
    Maple Orange-Banana Smoothie 24
    Parmesan Spinach Frittata 25
    Cottage Spinach Quiche 25
    Soybean-Flaxseed Granola 26
    Lemony Apple Granola Cobbler 27
    Apple Cereal Breakfast 27
    Grain Bowl with Fruit and Nuts 28
    Apple-Banana Smoothie 28
    Apple-Walnut Oatmeal 29
    Maple Pumpkin Custard 29
    Blueberry-Flaxseed Smoothie 30
    Almond Oat Groats 30
    Mango, Banana, and Pineapple Smoothie 31
    Perfect Pina Colada Smoothie 31
    Peanut Butter Blueberry Smoothie 31

Apple Granola with Sunflower Seeds 32

Chapter 2 Vegan and Vegetarian Recipes 33

Instant Pot Butternut Squash 33
Turmeric Coconut Rice 33
Lemony Spinach and White Beans 34
Scrambled Tofu 34
Garlic Lentil and Carrot Soup 35
Avocado, Beans, and Pepper Salad 35
Dijon Macaroni and Cheese 36
Parmesan Pasta with Peas and Tomatoes 36
Fried Rice with Awesome Sauce 37
Stuffed Avocado 37
Spinach and Beans with Rice 38
Black Beans and Tomato Soup 38
Awesome Brown Rice 39
Instant Pot Rice with Olives 39
Garlic Cauliflower 40
Balsamic Zucchini Kebabs 40
Carrot and Peas Salad 41
Avocado and Cucumber Soup 41
Carrot and Pepper with Cottage 42
Garlic Broccoli 42
Rosemary-Chickpea Omelet 43
Savory Baked Potatoes 43
Zuccchini and Beans Burrito 44

Chapter 3 Salad and Sides Recipes 45

Sautéed Zucchini 45
Healthy Apple, Spinach & Eggs Salad 45
Chickpeas, Onion, Tomato & Parsley in a Jar 46
Arugula, Carrot, Corn & Spinach in a Jar 46
Shrimp, Cucumber & Arugula 47
Tomato, Cucumber, Pumpkin & Dandelion 47
Carrot, Peppers, Cucumber & Cabbage 48
Tomato, Cucumber, Carrot & Parsley Salad 48
Apple Pepper Coleslaw 49
Chicken & Roasted Veggies Salad 49
Broccoli Seafood Salad 50
Tuna, Veggies & Eggs Salad 50
Easy Avocado, Tomato, Arugula Salad 51
Vegetable Chicken Salad 51
Easy Green Pomegranate Salad 52
Vegetable Salad in a Jar 52
Keto Cauliflower Rice 53

Sautéed Spinach 53
Artichoke Lamb Salad 54
Tuna, Eggs & Lettuce Salad 54
Creamy Cauliflower... 55

Chapter 4 Lunch Recipes 56

Walnut Mushroom Gravy 56
Avocado, Beans, and Nuts Salad... 56
Wrapped Bacon, Avocado, and Tomato with Basil-Mayo 57
Mozzarella Lasagna Rolls 57
Kale Garbanzo Burgers... 58
Lime Avocado Pasta 58
Basil Spelt Flatbread 59
Garlic Spaghetti with Bolognese Sauce 59
Mozzarella Margherita Pizza 60
Sautéed Zucchinis and Eggplants... 60
Macaroni and Cheese with Nuts 61
Vegan Pasta with Cheese and Peas 61
Mexican Steak Taco 62
Basil Pesto Noodles.. 62
Havarti Party Burgers... 63
Zucchini Noodles with Walnuts 63
Herbed Kamut Pasta 64
Awesome Jerk Patties 65
Cabbage Wraps with Strawberries and Nuts 66
Millet Tabbouleh with Cilantro 66
Balsamic Ground Beef.. 67
Mango, Quinoa, and Black Bean Casserole with Sauce 67
Fried Rice with Mushrooms and Zucchini 68
Ginger-Maple Yam Casserole.. 68
Gingered Zucchini Noodles 69
Garlic Chicken and Asparagus Fry 70
Stuffed Potato Cake 71

Chapter 5 Dinner Recipes 72

Quinoa-Fruit Bowl.. 72
Keto Avocado and Tahini Bowl.. 72
Stuffed Portobello Mushrooms 73
Popcorn Shrimp in Milk 74
Lemon Rosemary Salmon 74
Honey Zucchini and Leeks 75
Tofu Strips with Vegetables... 75
Fish Tacos 76
Chicken-Broccoli Stuffed Peppers 77
Veggie Beef Bacon Burgers 78

Quinoa Vegetable Bowl 78
Baby Courgettes in Vegetable Stock 79
Cucumber Shrimp 79
Seitan with Avocado Puree 80
Salmon Onion Stew 80
Grilled Tempeh and Pineapple with Vegetables 81
Sautéed Chicken Breast 81
Spring-Thyme Chicken Stew 82
Chorizo and Brown Rice Bowls 83
Salmon and Caramelized Veggies 84
Breaded Cod Fillets 85
Curry Chicken Breast with Potatoes 86
Veggie Skewers with Corn 87

Chapter 6 Snack and Appetizer Recipes 88

Tomato Muffin Pizzas 88
Shortbread Vanilla Cookies 88
Sautéed Banana Hash Browns 89
Homemade Zucchini Strips 89
Fried Sausage Links 90
Wheat Coconut Crackers 90
Za'atar Crackers 91
Simple Hemp Seed Porridge 91
Coconut Cacao Cookies 92
Coconut Millet Porridge 92
Spice Spelt Bread 93
Easy Mango Salsa 93
Quick Jackfruit Vegetable Fry 94
Maple Pistachios Ginger Mix 94
Blueberry-Strawberry Muffins 95
Squash Onion Hash 95
Jalapeño Zucchini Pancakes 96
Lime Avocado Gazpacho 96
Butternut Squash Patties 97
Blueberry Spelt Cakes 97
Mushroom Pasta with Onion 98

Conclusion 99

Appendix Measurement Conversion Chart 100

Introduction

The biggest challenge of any weight-loss diet plan is to stay consistent enough to actually see the visible results. It's natural to lose motivation to eat healthily and stay active when you cannot see yourself getting rid of those extra belly fats. The whole body reset program comes as a blessing in disguise for all those like me who want to achieve weight loss in a few days. The idea is to quickly switch to a healthy diet plan with limited calorie intake and exercise to kick start weight loss, and when that happens, the dieter then feels motivated to continue eating healthy. The science behind the whole body reset diet plan is deeper than that, and in this cookbook, I will explain it in depth. There are tons of whole-body-reset recipes in here that are going to help you through this dietary regimen.

Fundamentals of Whole Body Reset

Poor dietary habits, low metabolism, and an inactive lifestyle; there are several causes of weight gain, and you can blame any, but to counter them, all you need is the whole body reset. In today's world, we all are inclined to eat processed, unhealthy food, work late hours, and stay sleep-deprived with little-to-no regular exercise, and that cannot change unless we press that "reset" button and start making healthier choices. And that's what the whole body reset program is all about; it gives you the kick-start that you need to lose weight and become healthy as you want to be. It has proven to be a life-changer for me, and if you follow it as per the given guidelines, you can too achieve good results.

What is the Whole Body Reset?

With the first-ever tried-and-test, a science-based weight-reduction program created to shrink your belly, lengthen your life, and create your healthiest self in mid-life and beyond, you can stop and even reverse age-related weight gain and muscle loss. Age-related weight gain does not have to happen for you. That is a simple yet ground-breaking claim made by the proponents of this diet; it says that traditional diet and exercise stop working for us as we get older, and just small dietary changes can prevent and even cure age-related weight gain and muscle loss.

The whole body reset basically entails eating three meals per day that each contains 30 grams of protein (25 grams for women) and 5 grams of fiber, as well as one or two snacks that each contain 7 grams of protein and 2 grams of fiber. Meals should also include fruits, vegetables, nuts, and dairy products (for me, pea milk; you can be lactose-free, gluten-free, even vegan or vegetarian on this plan). In general, simply being more aware of what you are putting into your body will help you lose weight, have more energy, and be mentally sharper.

Stephen Perrine contributed to more than twenty New York Times bestsellers, including the Eat This, Not That! Series, as an author, editor, or publisher. He is in charge of the health and wellness coverage for AARP the Magazine and the AARP Bulletin, which is read by more than 38 million people. Together with Danica Patrick, he co-authored the book Pretty Intense. He also co-founded the nationally televised health and wellness program Better Man for males. Heidi Skolnik is a nutritionist and exercise physiologist who has been featured on numerous national television programs, including the Today show, Live! with Kelly and Michael, and the Food Network. She has been a part of the Women Sports Medicine Center at the Hospital for Special Surgery for more than 20 years and manages performance nutrition at the School of American Ballet and the Julliard School.

Together they came up with the whole body reset diet. According to them, the whole body reset presents startling new research that challenges conventional wisdom, dispels the fallacy of sluggish metabolisms and "inevitable" weight gain, and transforms how people in their mid-forties and older should view food. This research shows the power of "protein timing" for people in midlife. The proponents of this diet explain how our bodies change as we age and how eating protein-rich food support those changes, and it can help us respond to exercise as if we were 20 to 30 years younger.

By claiming to add a little exercise each day, this weight-loss program motivates you to move around. It suggests doing resistance exercises to stimulate muscle building in good water. It also suggests light resistance exercises, which will aid in muscular growth. The majority of specialists concur that a healthy weight loss plan should include both food adjustments and physical activity, and that's what this program recommends.

Protein Timing

The key to preventing weight gain at a later age is to time your protein intake or consume the proper amounts of protein throughout the day. This causes elderly bodies to resist fat storage and maintain lean muscle mass. This strategy, together with an abundance of vitamins, minerals, fiber, and good fats, can assist older individuals in reshaping not only their bodies but also their lives.

The Science of Protein Timing

We once thought that the reason we put on weight in middle age was due to a loss in metabolism, or more specifically, what scientists refer to as resting metabolic rate (RMR), which is the amount of energy your body requires to carry out basic processes. However, a startling study discovered that our individual cells continue to function roughly at the same rate in our 40s and 50s as they did in our 20s. In fact, our metabolic rate doesn't begin to slow until around age 60, when it starts to decline at a rate of 0.7 percent per year. Therefore, metabolism is not the cause of the expanding waistline you've noticed or the difference between your current and 20s-era bodies. Another factor plays its part here—something you have real control over the amount of protein you consume and how much you exercise. According to the whole body reset, the quality and amount of protein you consume at a later age makes all the difference.

According to studies, a younger individual can obtain the same amount of protein from only a few eggs while an older person can from at least 25 to 30 grams at a time. Muscle is continually being destroyed and rebuilt by the human body. However, muscular tissue gradually starts to disappear when long-term muscle breakdown outpaces long-term muscle repair. According to studies, older people who don't consume 25 to 30 grams of protein in the morning are more likely to continue losing muscle throughout the day. Adults start losing between 3 and 8 percent of their muscular mass per decade sometime between the ages of 30 and 40.

We develop more fat with the less muscle we have as we age. In addition to burning more calories, muscle also aids in blood sugar regulation. Your blood sugar will rise if you have lesser muscular mass, forcing your body to convert more of that blood sugar into fat. That is why losing muscle has been associated with a higher risk of diabetes, cancer, heart disease, Alzheimer's, and a weakened immune system.

It is because of this reason that the whole body reset diet suggests that as aging, a person must increase his protein intake so that his muscle would increase and keep the blood sugar in control while avoiding obesity and other ills that come with weight gain. A high protein intake must be coupled with some resistance exercises so that the muscle-building process in the body would speed up. It also helps to burn belly fat and extra calories, which really works best for weight loss.

The Advantages of Whole Body Reset

Weight loss is not the only health benefit that you are going to experience through the goodness of this dietary program; there are other advantages that make this diet plan a must to try. Let me name a few here:

Keep you Motivated.

Whatever weight you lose during this time may inspire you to continue the whole body reset diet for longer. This is due to the association between initial quick weight loss and long-term diet success. On the other hand, lower early weight loss is linked to higher weight-loss program dropout rates. Researchers hypothesize that motivation levels may be to blame for this disparity. Simply said, people may be more inspired to continue with the program if they see immediate results because they believe it works.

Simple to Follow.

The whole body reset diet involves some nutritional management. You must make sure that you consume more than 30 grams of protein per meal and the diet blueprint gives suggestions to reach that target. This diet offers the simplest of meal plans with lesser restrictions than other weight-loss regimes you have heard about.

Gain Increased Metabolic Rate.

Your ability to burn more calories may rise if you consume more protein. In contrast to the 5–15% rise in metabolic rate caused by digesting carbohydrates or fat, protein digestion appears to raise metabolic rate by an astonishing 20–35%. In fact, a number of studies have revealed that consuming a meal high in protein causes people to burn more calories for several hours thereafter. A high-protein diet for one day increases metabolic rate after meals about twice as much as a high-carb diet for one day.

Lose Weight and Improve Body Composition

It should come as no surprise that protein's capacity to boost metabolism, enhance fullness, and reduce hunger can aid in weight loss. Increased protein consumption encourages weight loss and fat loss, according to several high-quality research. 65 overweight and obese women participated in six-month diet research, and the high-protein group lost an average of 43% more fat than the high-carb group. Additionally, 35% of the female participants in the high-protein group shed at least 22 pounds (10 kg). Usually, your metabolism slows down when you eat fewer calories. Loss of muscle is one reason for this.

Nutritional Daily Meal of High Fiber and Healthy Fats.

By concentrating on healthy-fat foods while you're attempting to lose weight, you'll eat fewer calories. Greek yogurt with no added fat and skim milk are simple substitutions that the whole body reset diet recommends. The diet also puts a strong emphasis on eating enough fiber. It promotes the use of fruits and veggies, which is ideal for better fiber consumption. Fiber is essential for maintaining a healthy digestive system. Additionally, it could lower your risk of certain cancers. Smoothies are great for incorporating fiber-rich fruits and vegetables in large quantities. The whole body reset diet makes it simple for folks who might otherwise find it difficult to get enough fruit and fiber in their normal diet.

Guidelines of Whole Body Reset

This cookbook includes a 4-week diet plan helping through the whole body reset program. You will enter a maintenance phase after the 4-week diet plan, which means that you need to stick to healthy food to keep your weight loss maintained. It also emphasizes calories from high-fiber carbs, which it claims are found in pretty much every fruit, and protein, relying largely on milk protein for its smoothies. Here are all the guidelines that you need to follow to incorporate the whole body reset program into your lifestyle:

Consume 25 to 30 grams of high-quality protein.

The average American diet consists of a small amount of protein at breakfast, milk in your cereal, possibly an egg or two, a little bit more at lunch, possibly a turkey sandwich, and then a large amount of protein at dinner, a steak or a few pork chops. In total, we might eat around 90 grams of protein per day, which is about what we require. But often, two-thirds of that occurs at dinner. To keep the process of protein production running smoothly, our bodies require 25 to 30 grams of protein at each meal, typically 25 grams for women and 30 grams for men. Our systems may only be able to use roughly 30 grams of protein at a time when at rest, so eating too much protein for supper doesn't help. The foods rich in protein include fish and shellfish, eggs, chicken, lean meat, combos of whole grains and legumes, and protein drinks. You can consume any of those ingredients 2-4 times each day.

Dairy is the great choice of complete protein. And the advantages of dairy products like milk, cheese, yogurt, and others only increase with age. That's partly because dairy packs a powerful protein punch and contains particularly high levels of leucine, a substance crucial for building muscle. However, dairy also contains a variety of other minerals, most notably calcium, magnesium, and vitamin D, all of which our bodies find more challenging to absorb from food as we age and all of which support our physical and mental well-being. Increased consumption of milk, yogurt, and cheese was linked to both increased muscle mass and grip strength in a study of older women. Food that is rich in protein includes smoothies with whey-based protein, cheese, milk, yogurt, and kefir that have been fortified with vitamin D.

Consume 5 grams of fiber per meal.

You probably don't consume enough fiber. The average American consumes almost 15 grams of fiber a day, which is about the same amount as any of these:

- 1 cup of black beans
- 2 cups bran flakes
- 3 muffins with oat bran
- 5 bananas
- 10 carrots
- 13 servings of popcorn

And it only makes up roughly ½ of the recommended daily intake recommended by experts for maintaining maximum health and a leaner, fitter body. The dietary habits of middle-aged women were investigated in one study. Twenty months later, the researchers discovered that the subjects' total weight and fat content reduced by half a pound and by a quarter of a percentage point for every extra gram of fiber they consumed. The fiber-rich food that you should consume includes whole-wheat pasta, bread, crackers, and tortillas, as well as oats, brown rice, beans, vegetables like broccoli, corn, Brussels sprouts, peas, and potatoes (still with the skin on), and fruits.

All vegetables are healthy to eat on this diet, as long as they aren't breaded or deep-fried in oil—it helps to think of dark, leafy greens as the king of the vegetable kingdom. A small salad or a half-cup serving of cooked green vegetables should be consumed at least once a day to ensure that you get a dietary source of the B vitamin folate. Folate is also essential for older persons' fights against dementia, hearing loss, and depression.

In a study of postmenopausal women, those who were overweight or obese had blood levels of folate that were on average 12 percent lower than those of normal-weight women. All types of colorful fruits and vegetables, but especially dark, leafy greens (lettuce, spinach, and kale), cruciferous vegetables (cauliflower, broccoli, arugula, cabbage, Brussels sprouts, collards, and watercress), red and orange vegetables (carrots, squash, red peppers, tomatoes), berries, tree fruits (apples, pears, and cherries), and citrus, are among the top foods (oranges, grapefruit, lemons, limes).

Healthy Fats

I have one piece of advice for anyone who has been trying to reduce weight by consuming less fat: to stop. There are actually three different kinds of healthy fats that you ought to consume more of. The first one is fatty acids omega-3. These beneficial fats, which may be found in fish like salmon, mackerel, sardines, and tuna, have been demonstrated to help older adults lose abdominal fat and preserve muscle mass. The second is nut and fruit oils. According to studies, extra-virgin olive oil may lower the incidence of dementia by clearing the brain cells' communication pathways of the proteins that clog them. The third one is milk fat. Full-fat dairy products have been associated with a lower risk of obesity. That may be partially due to the fact that satiating creamy fats decrease the urge to nibble later. The sources of healthy fats that you should consider include olives, avocados, nuts, seeds, seafood, oils (olive, safflower, peanut, sesame), and seeds.

Foods to Avoid

The whole-body-reset dietary program is not restrictive in the sense that it does not stop you from eating any particular food group. Rather it suggests focusing on healthier food. But there are certain food products that may reserve the effect of the whole weight loss efforts you make by following this program.

Sweetened Beverages

Food items with added sugar must be avoided, such as sugar-loaded food like drinks, sweets, and candies. Beverages are a substantial source of empty calories. Sugar can be found in soda, sweetened iced tea, specialized coffee drinks, sports drinks, oversized smoothies and shakes, and even fruit juices. Instead of consuming regular sugar, focus on using organic sweeteners in your food. Lastly, the amount of fat, proteins, and carbs you add to your food mainly matters here. If there is too much sugar in the food, your body will turn the excess into fats, and you will never be able to achieve weight loss. So make sure to consume more proteins, healthy fats, and a moderate amount of complex carbs while avoiding too many refined carbs.

Added Sugar

An increase in insulin is brought on by extra sugar, and when insulin levels are high, your body stores fat rather than burns it. Refined carbs can cause a "crash and burn effect," which increases appetite, "hanger," and cravings as blood sugar levels fall below the optimal range. The bad news is that 80 percent of our food supply has added sugar. The positive news is that all the things that contain added sugar are usually found in one section, which is often the center of your supermarket, where the packaged items take up most of the space. The best course of action is to "shop the perimeter," where you may concentrate on fresh produce and natural, whole foods. Stick to your list, examine labels, the contents of even similar products can vary greatly, and avoid shopping when you're hungry.

Highly Processed Foods

What foods are considered to be highly processed? They are the "corporate concoctions" that are frequently found in the center of the supermarket. Frequently, they contain five or more ingredients. If any of those ingredients are difficult for you to pronounce, the food you are holding in your hand is probably highly processed. In reality, they are so heavily processed that they offer no true nutritional advantages.

Dietary Tips for the Whole Body Reset

Consult a nutritionist and ask for professional advice for yourself.

Your body type, metabolic rate, and health condition are all those factors that decide your overall protein needs. Instead of deciding it yourself, I must suggest you consult a nutritionist and talk to her about health and the whole body reset diet. The suggestions from an expert always help.

Make diet plans for nutritional choices and to avoid unexpected habits.

Making wise nutritional choices is also encouraged by the diet. Making a set schedule and eating routine is necessary to prevent the temptation to eat unhealthy snacks when you're hungry and to improve your eating efficiency by making every calorie count.

Keep record of the protein and fiber sources to maintain your healthy lifestyle.

Try to add as many healthy protein and fiber sources to your diet as you can.

Don't go tough on yourself.

If you are not habitual in doing exercises, then start with a light resistance workout and work your way up to the tougher exercises. It is the regularity of the physical exercises that matter here.

Ensure the daily protein consumption.

Besides the entrees, make sure to add proteins to your snacks as well. Having roasted nuts, chickpeas, beef jerky, or a glass of protein smoothie are some the great ideas to increase your protein consumption.

Keep exercises for your muscles.

Remember, consuming too many proteins without doing the exercises can cause more harm than good; the more the muscles work, the more quickly they utilize the protein provided through diet.

FAQS

Is too much protein consumption bad for health?

Yes, there are some risk factors. If you suddenly start consuming too much protein, it can affect your health negatively. Most people can comfortably consume a diet high in protein, at least temporarily. While some studies suggest that increased protein intake may harm the kidneys, another study demonstrates that individuals with healthy kidneys won't have any detrimental effects. Clinical research does, however, indicate that those with renal illness shouldn't consume a high-protein diet. Similar to this, it appears that those who are prone to kidney stones should stay away from high-protein diets, especially those that contain a lot of animal proteins. Before starting a high-protein diet, people with other medical issues should consult a healthcare provider. It's crucial to keep in mind that there is currently no research examining the long-term impact of high-protein diets on general health, despite the fact that short-term studies suggest that they can promote weight loss.

Does the whole body reset diet have any other health risks?

Although the whole body reset diet has no known health risks, you should always speak with a doctor if you have a health risk before making any significant dietary changes. I generally suggest to everyone talk to an expert before deciding on a new dietary plan for themselves. The advice from a certified expert is always better than randomly reading things off the internet.

Does the whole Body Reset Diet promote heart health?

Because the whole body reset diet has not been the subject of any scientific research, it is uncertain. The whole body reset diet, on the other hand, emphasizes healthy meals with a focus on fruits and vegetables, protein, healthy fats, and exercise, which is always good news for heart health. During the 4-week diet plan, you're on a diet, you'll avoid or at least limit processed foods, but if you keep up this eating pattern over time, you might benefit your heart.

Can the whole body reset diet help to manage or prevent diabetes?

One of the largest risk factors for Type 2 diabetes is being overweight. You'll almost surely improve your chances of avoiding diabetes if the whole body reset diet helps you lose weight and keep it off. It's not apparent if the whole body reset diet aids in managing diabetes. Before starting the diet, discuss the diet plan with your doctor because fruits, vegetables, and yogurt might be rich in sugar.

Is the whole body reset diet nutritious?

Yes, it practically suggests you eat more protein, healthy fats, and complex carbs. There is nothing that you cannot eat on this diet except added sugar and processed food, and that means this diet is nothing but nutritious. It can magically transform your bad eating habit and put you on a path that can keep you forever healthy, active, and young.

Will the whole body reset diet help you lose weight?

Yes, if you follow the three meals per day meal plan with more proteins and less sugar, you can definitely achieve weight loss. Just make sure not to skip the daily exercise if you really want to see a difference in your waistline. You can only lose weight by burning down the body fats and building more muscles, and following this diet for 4 weeks or more can really help you achieve that.

Is the whole body reset diet too costly?

No, the whole body reset diet will require you to purchase all the food that you already buy, like a lot of fruits and vegetables. There is no fancy and high-priced product that you might need to use on this diet. In fact, on this diet, you will avoid a lot of processed products which will cut down your grocery spending significantly.

4-Week Diet Plan

This 4-Week Diet Plan is created to show a simple example. You can follow this to your diet or learn to build your own fare under the instruction of the brief introduction in this cookbook. Just keep the simple tenets below in mind and remember that meal plan may differ from personal favored tastes to physical condition. Start your healthy life by following this diet and take control your life from now on!

For Men:

- Breakfast: at least 30 grams of protein and at least 5 grams of fiber, about 500-550 calories.
- Lunch: at least 30 grams of protein and at least 5 grams of fiber, about 550 calories.
- Dinner: at least 30 grams of protein and at least 5 grams of fiber, about 400-500 calories
- Snacks: at least 7 grams of protein and at least 2 grams of fiber, 250-300 calories.

For Women:

- Breakfast: at least 25 grams of protein and at least 5 grams of fiber, about 350-450 calories.
- Lunch: at least 25 grams of protein and at least 5 grams of fiber, about 450-500 calories.
- Dinner: at least 25 grams of protein and at least 5 grams of fiber, about 400-500 calories
- Snacks: at least 7 grams of protein and at least 2 grams of fiber, 250-300 calories.

Week 1

Day 1:
Breakfast: Spanish Sausage Tortilla
Lunch: Scrambled Tofu
Snack: Spice Spelt Bread
Dinner: Tofu Strips with Vegetables

Day 2:
Breakfast: Sweet Potatoes and Cheese Ole
Lunch: Zucchini and Beans Burrito
Snack: Blueberry-Strawberry Muffins
Dinner: Curry Chicken Breast with Potatoes

Day 3:
Breakfast: Maple Pumpkin Custard
Lunch: Rosemary-Chickpea Omelet
Snack: Za'atar Crackers
Dinner: Salmon and Caramelized Veggies

Day 4:
Breakfast: Rosemary-Chickpea Omelet
Lunch: Spinach and Beans with Rice
Snack: Coconut Millet Porridge
Dinner: Chorizo and Brown Rice Bowls

Day 5:
Breakfast: Almond Oat Groats
Lunch: Tuna, Veggies & Eggs Salad
Snack: Peanut Butter Blueberry Smoothie
Dinner: Fish Tacos

Day 6:

Breakfast: Cottage Spinach Quiche
Lunch: Tuna, Eggs & Lettuce Salad
Snack: Refreshing Papaya Smoothie
Dinner: Veggie Beef Bacon Burgers

Day 7:
Breakfast: Spanish Sausage Tortilla
Lunch: Garlic Spaghetti with Bolognese Sauce
Snack: 1 medium apple with 1 ounce cheddar cheese
Dinner: Seitan with Avocado Puree

Week 2

Day 1:
Breakfast: Soybean-Flaxseed Granola
Lunch: Lime Avocado Pasta
Snack: ⅓ cup hummus with sliced carrot, cucumber, and red bell pepper
Dinner: Tofu Strips with Vegetables

Day 2:
Breakfast: Almond Oat Groats
Lunch: Stuffed Potato Cake
Snack: ½ cup Greek yogurt with 1 cup blackberries and ¼ cup almonds
Dinner: Zucchini and Beans Burrito

Day 3:
Breakfast: Maple Pumpkin Custard
Lunch: Cabbage Wraps with Strawberries and Nuts
Snack: 1 medium banana with 2 tablespoons peanut butter
Dinner: Rosemary-Chickpea Omelet

Day 4:
Breakfast: Sweet Potatoes and Cheese Ole
Lunch: Awesome Jerk Patties
Snack: 1 medium apple with 1 ounce cheddar cheese
Dinner: Shrimp, Cucumber & Arugula

Day 5:
Breakfast: Spanish Sausage Tortilla
Lunch: Herbed Kamut Pasta
Snack: 1 medium banana with 2 tablespoons peanut butter
Dinner: Artichoke Lamb Salad

Day 6:
Breakfast: Cottage Spinach Quiche
Lunch: Mozzarella Lasagna Rolls
Snack: ⅓ cup hummus with sliced carrot, cucumber, and red bell pepper
Dinner: Chicken & Roasted Veggies Salad

Day 7:
Breakfast: Soybean-Flaxseed Granola
Lunch: Wrapped Bacon, Avocado, and Tomato with Basil-Mayo
Snack: trail mix of 2 tablespoons tart cherries, 2 tablespoons cashews, 20 pistachios, and ¼ cup wheat squares cereal
Dinner: Tuna, Veggies & Eggs Salad

Week 3

Day 1:
Breakfast: Almond Oat Groats
Lunch: Cabbage Wraps with Strawberries and Nuts
Snack: 2 medium celery stalks, 2 tablespoons almond butter, 1 small apple
Dinner: Tuna, Eggs & Lettuce Salad

Day 2:
Breakfast: Spanish Sausage Tortilla
Lunch: Avocado, Beans, and Nuts Salad
Snack: trail mix of 2 tablespoons tart cherries, 2 tablespoons cashews, 20 pistachios, and ¼ cup wheat squares cereal
Dinner: Grilled Tempeh and Pineapple with Vegetables

Day 3:
Breakfast: Apple Granola with Sunflower Seeds
Lunch: Kale Garbanzo Burgers
Snack: 1 medium banana with 2 tablespoons peanut butter
Dinner: Chorizo and Brown Rice Bowls

Day 4:
Breakfast: Soybean-Flaxseed Granola
Lunch: Mozzarella Margherita Pizza
Snack: 2 medium celery stalks, 2 tablespoons almond butter, 1 small apple
Dinner: Grilled Tempeh and Pineapple with Vegetables

Day 5:
Breakfast: Cottage Spinach Quiche
Lunch: Kale Garbanzo Burgers
Snack: ⅓ cup hummus with sliced carrot, cucumber, and red bell pepper
Dinner: Seitan with Avocado Puree

Day 6:
Breakfast: Almond Oat Groats
Lunch: Basil Spelt Flatbread
Snack: 1 medium banana with 2 tablespoons peanut butter
Dinner: Stuffed Portobello Mushrooms

Day 7:
Breakfast: Spanish Sausage Tortilla
Lunch: Cabbage Wraps with Strawberries and Nuts
Snack: ⅓ cup hummus with sliced carrot, cucumber, and red bell pepper
Dinner: Quinoa-Fruit Bowl

Week 4

Day 1:
Breakfast: Cottage Spinach Quiche
Lunch: Awesome Jerk Patties
Snack: 1 medium apple with 1 ounce cheddar cheese
Dinner: Seitan with Avocado Puree

Day 2:
Breakfast: Maple Pumpkin Custard
Lunch: Mozzarella Margherita Pizza
Snack: trail mix of 2 tablespoons tart cherries, 2 tablespoons cashews, 20 pistachios, and ¼ cup wheat squares cereal
Dinner: Tofu Strips with Vegetables

Day 3:
Breakfast: Spanish Sausage Tortilla
Lunch: Kale Garbanzo Burgers
Snack: ½ cup Greek yogurt with 1 cup blackberries and ¼ cup almonds
Dinner: Seitan with Avocado Puree

Day 4:
Breakfast: Cottage Spinach Quiche
Lunch: Avocado, Beans, and Nuts Salad
Snack: ⅓ cup hummus with sliced carrot, cucumber, and red bell pepper
Dinner: Quinoa-Fruit Bowl

Day 5:
Breakfast: Almond Oat Groats
Lunch: Cabbage Wraps with Strawberries and Nuts
Snack: 1 medium banana with 2 tablespoons peanut butter
Dinner: Breaded Cod Fillets

Day 6:
Breakfast: Soybean-Flaxseed Granola
Lunch: Garlic Spaghetti with Bolognese Sauce
Snack: ½ cup Greek yogurt with 1 cup blackberries and ¼ cup almonds
Dinner: Fish Tacos

Day 7:
Breakfast: Sweet Potatoes and Cheese Ole
Lunch: Garlic Chicken and Asparagus Fry
Snack: trail mix of 2 tablespoons tart cherries, 2 tablespoons cashews, 20 pistachios, and ¼ cup wheat squares cereal
Dinner: Salmon and Caramelized Veggies

Chapter 1 Breakfast and Smoothie Recipes

Spinach-Pear Smoothie

Prep time: 10 minutes| **Cook time:** 5 minutes| **Serves:** 5

2 cups spinach leaves, packed
1 ripe pear, peeled, cored, and chopped
15 green or red grapes
6 ounces fat-free plain Greek yogurt
2 tablespoons chopped avocado
1 or 2 tablespoons fresh lime juice

In a blender or food processor, combine the spinach leaves, pear, grapes, yogurt, avocado, and lime juice until blended to the desired consistency.

Per Serving: Calories 59; Fat 0.7g; Sodium 23mg; Carbs 10.3g; Fiber 2g; Sugar 7g; Protein 4g

Slow-Cooked Granola

Prep time: 10 minutes| **Cook time:** 3 to 8 hours| **Serves:** 10 to 12

5 cups gluten-free rolled oats
1 tablespoon flaxseeds
¼ cup slivered almonds
¼ cup chopped pecans or walnuts
¼ cup unsweetened shredded coconut
¼ cup maple syrup or honey
½ cup dried fruit
¼ cup melted coconut oil

Prepare the crock of the slow cooker and spray the inside with cooking spray. Combine oats, flaxseeds, almonds, pecans or walnuts, and coconut in a slow cooker.
Combine maple syrup or honey and coconut oil separately. Toss the dry ingredients in the cooker with the liquid.
Cover the lid and vent one end of the lid with a wooden spoon handle or chopstick.
Cook for 3–4 hours on high, stirring every 30 minutes, or 8 hours on low, stirring every hour. Depending on how hot your cooker cooks, you may need to stir more frequently or cook for shorter time.
Pour the Granola onto a baking sheet to cool when it smells delicious and toasty.
Combine the dried fruit with the chilled Granola and store in an airtight container.

Per Serving: Calories 196; Fat 10g; Sodium 6mg; Carbs 34g; Fiber 7g; Sugar 6.8g; Protein 7.7g

Carrot-Peach Soup with Nuts

Prep time: 45 minutes| **Cook time:** 1 hour| **Serves:** 8

2 medium carrots, peeled and sliced
½-inch piece of peeled ginger, sliced
¾ cup plain Greek yogurt
¾ cup coconut milk
3 teaspoons fresh lime juice
12–15 peaches, skins removed, cut into ½-inch pieces
3–4 oranges, squeezed for juice to make ¾ cup
dash of sea salt
dash of cayenne pepper
⅛ teaspoon curry powder
2 tablespoons fresh chopped mint
¾ cup cashews or sliced almonds, finely chopped, optional

In your crock, combine the carrots and ginger and cook on high for 1 hour, or until the carrots and ginger are soft.
Blend the contents of the crock in a blender until smooth, and then set aside to chill.
Toss in the other ingredients, minus the nuts, into the blender mixture. Puree until completely smooth.
If preferred, garnish with chopped cashews or sliced almonds.
Serving suggestion: Garnish with fresh mint.

Per Serving: Calories 340; Fat 19g; Sodium 112mg; Carbs 41g; Fiber 6g; Sugar 30g; Protein 8.6g

Banana-Yam Smoothie

Prep time: 15 minutes| **Cook time:** 5 minutes| **Serves:** 7

2 medium yams
3 cups vanilla yogurt
1 cup milk
2 cups ice cubes
1 teaspoon white sugar
1 ripe banana, sliced

Prick yams with a fork, and place them on a plate. Cook in the microwave for 8 to 10 minutes, turning once, until tender. Cool, peel, and dice.
Then combine the yams, milk, ice cubes, sugar, and banana in the container of a blender. Blend until smooth.

Per Serving: Calories 132; Fat 4.6g; Sodium 74mg; Carbs 18g; Fiber 1.5g; Sugar 11.3g; Protein 5g

Sweet and Sour Raspberry Smoothie

Prep time: 5 minutes| **Cook time:** 3 minutes| **Serves:** 6

2 cups limeade
1 cup key pie yogurt
2 cups frozen raspberries
1 lime, sliced for garnish

Place the limeade, key pie yogurt, and raspberries into a blender (liquid ingredients first).
Blend on high power for 2 minutes or until smooth.
Then scrape down sides and continue blending for 30 seconds.
Serve and enjoy!

Per Serving: Calories 158; Fat 1.5g; Sodium 23mg; Carbs 36g; Fiber 3.8g; Sugar 32g; Protein 2g

Citrusy Berry Smoothie

Prep time: 10 minutes| **Cook time:** 5 minutes| **Serves:** 5

¾ cup fresh or frozen raspberries
¾ cup fresh or frozen pitted cherries
½ to ¾ cup fat-free milk, almond milk, or soy milk
1 orange, peeled
2 tablespoons vanilla or unflavored protein powder

In a blender or food processor, combine the raspberries, cherries, milk, orange, and vanilla. Blend until the mixture reaches your desired consistency.

Per Serving: Calories 89; Fat 0.2g; Sodium 17mg; Carbs 18g; Fiber 3g; Sugar 15g; Protein 1.6g

Refreshing Papaya Smoothie

Prep time: 15 minutes| **Cook time:** 5 minutes| **Serves:** 3

1 cup almond milk
½ cup fresh papaya
1 scoop protein powder
1-inch fresh turmeric root, peeled and chopped
½ inch fresh ginger root, peeled
3 ice cubes, or as desired

Combine almond milk, papaya, protein powder, turmeric root, and ginger root in a blender. Add ice and blend until smooth.

Per Serving: Calories 104; Fat 3.8g; Sodium 59mg; Carbs 11g; Fiber 1.2g; Sugar 7g; Protein 7g

Grain, Nuts, and Fruit Cereal

Prep time: 5 minutes| **Cook time:** 3 hours| **Serves:** 4 to 5

⅓ cup uncooked quinoa
⅓ cup uncooked millet
⅓ cup uncooked brown rice
4 cups water
¼ teaspoon salt
½ cup raisins or dried cranberries
¼ cup chopped nuts, optional
1 teaspoon vanilla extract, optional
½ teaspoon ground cinnamon, optional
1 tablespoon maple syrup, optional

Thoroughly rinse the quinoa, millet, and brown rice.
In a slow cooker, combine the grains, water, and salt. Cook on low for 3 hours, or until most of the water has been absorbed.
Then the dried fruit and any extra additions and cook for 30 minutes. Add a bit more water if the mixture is too thick.
Serve warm or chilled. Before serving, pour a little amount of non-dairy milk into each bowl of cereal.

Per Serving: Calories 235; Fat 6.8g; Sodium 123mg; Carbs 40g; Fiber 4g; Sugar 10.8g; Protein 4.6g

Morning Oatmeal

Prep time: 10 minutes| **Cook time:** 2½–6 hours| **Serves:** 6

1 cup uncooked gluten-free steel-cut oats
1 cup dried cranberries
1 cup walnuts
½ teaspoon kosher salt
1 tablespoon cinnamon
2 cups water
2 cups fat-free non-dairy milk (almond, rice, etc.)

In a slow cooker, add all of the dry ingredients and combine well. Stir everything together thoroughly.
Stir in the water and milk.
Put a cover over it. Cook for 2 ½ hours on high or 5–6 hours on low.

Per Serving: Calories 220; Fat 10g; Sodium 240mg; Carbs 34g; Fiber 10g; Sugar 17.7g; Protein 7.6g

Sweet Potatoes and Cheese Ole

Prep time: 10 minutes| **Cook time:** 6 hours| **Serves:** 8

4 pounds sweet potatoes, peeled and diced
1 15-ounce can black beans, drained, rinsed
1 cup chopped onion
1 4-ounce can diced green chilies
8 eggs
½ cup salsa
½ cup shredded Monterey Jack cheese

Coat the crock with non-stick cooking spray.
Combine sweet potatoes, black beans, onion, and diced green chilies in a crock.
Combine the eggs, salsa, and Monterey Jack cheese in a mixing bowl. Over the sweet potatoes, pour the sauce.
Cook on low for 6 hours, covered.

Per Serving: Calories 417; Fat 14.6g; Sodium 799mg; Carbs 58g; Fiber 13g; Sugar 12.8g; Protein 17.5g

Mexican Ranch-style Eggs

Prep time: 25 minutes| **Cook time:** 2 hours| **Serves:** 6

3 cups gluten-free salsa, room temperature
2 cups cooked beans, drained, room temperature
6 eggs, room temperature
salt and pepper to taste
⅓ cup grated Mexican-blend cheese, optional
6 white corn tortillas, for serving

In a slow cooker, combine the salsa and beans.
Cook for 1 hour on high, or until steaming.
Make 6 evenly spaced dents in the salsa mixture with a spoon, being careful not to expose the bottom of the crock. Each dent should be filled with an egg.
Season eggs with salt and pepper. If desired, top with grated cheese.
Cover and simmer on high for 20–40 minutes, or until egg whites are set and yolks are as hard as you like them.
To serve, scoop out an egg and place it on a plate with beans and salsa. Serve with tortillas that are still warm.

Per Serving: Calories 207; Fat 7.2g; Sodium 188mg; Carbs 26g; Fiber 3g; Sugar 1.8g; Protein 10g

Spanish Sausage Tortilla

Prep time: 25 minutes| **Cook time:** 5 to 6 hours| **Serves:** 6

1 pound turkey sausage, browned, drained
1 4.5-ounce package tostada shells, broken coarsely
1 medium red bell pepper, chopped
1 medium onion, chopped
1 4-ounce can diced green chilies
1 cup almond milk
12 eggs
1 teaspoon sea salt
¼ teaspoon black pepper
½ cup crumbled queso fresco
Optional toppings: 2 sliced avocados, 8 ounces non-fat Greek yogurt, 2 cups salsa

Coat the crock with non-stick cooking spray.
Toss browned sausage, tostada pieces, red bell pepper, onion, and green chilies together in a crock.
Combine the almond milk, eggs, sea salt, and black pepper in a large mixing dish.
On top of the sausage mixture in the crock, pour the egg mixture.
Scatter crumbled queso fresco on top.
Cook on low for 5–6 hours, covered. Garnish with Pico de Gallo.

Per Serving: Calories 503; Fat 27.7g; Sodium 1835mg; Carbs 37g; Fiber 8.8g; Sugar 5.6g; Protein 31g

Maple Orange-Banana Smoothie

Prep time: 15 minutes| **Cook time:** 15 minutes| **Serves:** 5

10 ice cubes
1 banana
4 teaspoons maple syrup
4 teaspoons brown sugar
1 cup eggnog
¼ cup orange juice
¼ cup vanilla yogurt

Blend the ice, banana, maple syrup, brown sugar, eggnog, orange juice, and vanilla yogurt together in a blender until smooth.

Per Serving: Calories 107; Fat 2.6g; Sodium 35mg; Carbs 18.6g; Fiber 0.7g; Sugar 15.3g; Protein 3g

Parmesan Spinach Frittata

Prep time: 15 minutes| **Cook time:** 1½–2 hours| **Serves:** 4 to 6

4 eggs
½ teaspoon kosher salt
½ teaspoon dried basil
fresh ground pepper, to taste
3 cups chopped fresh spinach, stems removed
½ cup chopped tomato, liquid drained off
⅓ cup freshly grated Parmesan cheese

In a mixing basin, whisk the eggs thoroughly. Combine the salt, basil, and pepper in a mixing bowl.
Stir in the spinach, tomato, and Parmesan cheese gently.
Pour into a lightly greased slow cooker.
Cook on high for 1 ½–2 hours, or until the middle is set. Serve immediately.

Per Serving: Calories 115; Fat 4.8g; Sodium 464mg; Carbs 8.6g; Fiber 1.5g; Sugar 3.5g; Protein 10g

Cottage Spinach Quiche

Prep time: 15 minutes| **Cook time:** 2 to 4 hours| **Serves:** 8

2 10-ounce packages frozen chopped spinach
2 cups cottage cheese
¼ cup coconut oil
1½ cups sharp cheddar cheese, cubed
3 eggs, beaten
¼ cup all-purpose gluten-free flour
1 teaspoon salt

Prepare the slow cooker and grease the inside.
Thoroughly defrost the spinach. Squeeze out as much moisture as you can. Then put it in a crock.
Combine the cottage cheese, coconut oil, cheddar cheese, 3 eggs, flour, and salt in a large mixing bowl.
Cook on low for 2–4 hours, or until the quiche has set. Knife blade should be inserted into the center of the quiche. If the knife comes out clean, the quiche is ready. If it doesn't, cover and cook for an additional 15 minutes.
Allow 10–15 minutes for the mixture to firm up once it has been cooked. After that, serve.

Per Serving: Calories 269; Fat 19g; Sodium 717mg; Carbs 8g; Fiber 2g; Sugar 2g; Protein 16.8g

Soybean-Flaxseed Granola

Prep time: 20 minutes| **Cook time:** 1½–2½ hours| **Serves:** 15

12 ounces soybeans, roasted with no salt
4 cups gluten-free rolled oats
¾ cup soy flour
¾ cup ground flaxseeds
1 teaspoon salt
2 teaspoons cinnamon
⅔ cup coarsely chopped walnuts
⅔ cup whole pecans
¾ cup maple syrup
½ cup coconut oil, melted
¾ cup applesauce
2 teaspoons vanilla
Optional additions: dried cranberries, dried cherries, chopped dried apricots, chopped dried figs, raisins, or some combination of these dried fruits

Prepare the slow cooker and lightly grease the inside.
Pulse the soybeans in a blender or a food processor until finely chopped. Place in a large mixing basin.
Combine the oats, flour, flaxseeds, salt, cinnamon, walnuts, and pecans in a mixing bowl. With a spoon, thoroughly combine the ingredients.
Whisk together maple syrup, coconut oil, applesauce, and vanilla in a smaller mixing dish.
Combine wet and dry ingredients in a mixing bowl. Using a strong spoon or your clean hands, stir well, remembering to stir up from the bottom.
Pour the mixture into the crock pot. Leave the lid open with a chopstick or wooden spoon handle to allow steam to escape. Turn the lid sideways if you're using an oval cooker.
Cook for 1 hour on high, stirring occasionally from the bottom and around the edges about 20 minutes. (Don't forget to set a timer!)
Reduce the heat to low. Continue baking for another 1–2 hours, stirring every 20 minutes.
When the granola starts to brown and looks dry, it's done.
Spread the granola out on parchment paper or a big baking sheet to cool and crisp up.
Add in as many dried fruits as you'd like.
If you prefer clumps, don't stir the granola again while it cools. Otherwise, when the granola cools, break it up with a spoon or your hands.
Place in an airtight jar once entirely cool.

Per Serving: Calories 397; Fat 25g; Sodium 198mg; Carbs 41.5g; Fiber 11.6g; Sugar 12.8g; Protein 16g

Lemony Apple Granola Cobbler

Prep time: 25 minutes| **Cook time:** 2 to 9 hours| **Serves:** 8

8 medium apples, cored, peeled, sliced
2 tablespoons maple syrup
dash of cinnamon
juice of 1 lemon
2 tablespoons coconut oil, melted
2 cups homemade granola

In a slow cooker, add the apples, maple syrup, cinnamon, lemon juice, coconut oil, and the granola.
Put a cover over it. Cook on low for 7-9 hours (while you sleep!) or high for 2-3 hours (after you wake up).

Per Serving: Calories 221; Fat 8.5g; Sodium 32mg; Carbs 37g; Fiber 5g; Sugar 25.7g; Protein 2g

Apple Cereal Breakfast

Prep time: 10 minutes| **Cook time:** 6 to 7 hours| **Serves:** 10 cups

5 cups water
2 cups seven-grain cereal
1 medium apple, peeled and chopped
1 cup unsweetened apple juice
¼ cup dried apricots, chopped
¼ cup dried cranberries
¼ cup raisins
¼ cup chopped dates
¼ cup maple syrup
1 teaspoon cinnamon
½ teaspoon salt
Chopped walnuts, optional

Combine all ingredients in the crock except the walnuts.
Cook on low for 6-7 hours, or until fruits are softened, with the lid covered.
If preferred, top individual servings with walnuts.

Per Serving (per cup)**:** Calories 124; Fat 0.5g; Sodium 164mg; Carbs 31g; Fiber 2.8g; Sugar 18g; Protein 1.7g

Grain Bowl with Fruit and Nuts

Prep time: 15 minutes| **Cook time:** 6 to 7 hours| **Serves:** 8

5 cups water
1 cup dried fruit and nuts (cranberries, cherries, raisins, pineapple, coconut, pecans, and/or walnuts)
¼ cup crystalized ginger
3 tablespoons gluten-free oats
3 tablespoons quinoa
3 tablespoons brown rice
2 tablespoons flaxseeds
2 tablespoons gluten-free cornmeal
1 teaspoon vanilla
1 teaspoon cinnamon
1 tablespoon hemp seeds, optional
Optional toppings: milk, yogurt, turbinado sugar, maple syrup, honey

Prepare your slow cooker and coat the inside with nonstick cooking spray.
In a slow cooker, combine all ingredients (excluding optional toppings), cover, and cook on low for 6–7 hours.
If preferred, top with any of the alternative toppings. If you want to keep the recipe vegan, don't use dairy milk, yogurt, or honey as toppings.

Per Serving: Calories 159; Fat 8.7g; Sodium 6mg; Carbs 17.7g; Fiber 3g; Sugar 4g; Protein 5g

Apple-Banana Smoothie

Prep time: 5 minutes| **Cook time:** 5 minutes| **Serves:** 4

5 raw almonds, whole or chopped
1 red apple, unpeeled, cored and chopped
4 fluid-ounces fat-free natural Greek yogurt
6½ ounces skimmed milk
½ teaspoon ground cinnamon, or to taste
1 small frozen banana, frozen and cut into chunks

Blend the almonds until they are fully ground. (If your blender isn't powerful enough to grind almonds, you can buy chopped almonds or even ground almonds instead.)
Add the apple, banana, yogurt, milk, and cinnamon. Blend together the mixture until it reaches the consistency you desired.

Per Serving: Calories 106; Fat 2.4g; Sodium 39mg; Carbs 19.6g; Fiber 3.4g; Sugar 11.7g; Protein 3g

Apple-Walnut Oatmeal

Prep time: 20 minutes| **Cook time:** 3 to 5 hours| **Serves:** 5

2 cups fat-free milk
1 cup water
1 tablespoon honey
1 tablespoon coconut oil
¼ teaspoon kosher salt
½ teaspoon cinnamon
1 cup gluten-free steel-cut oats
1 cup chopped apples
½ cup chopped walnuts
1 tablespoon turbinado sugar

Prepare the crock and coat the interior with cooking spray.
Combine all ingredients in a crock and stir well.
Put a cover over it. Cook for 3–5 hours on low.

Per Serving: Calories 189; Fat 9g; Sodium 170mg; Carbs 27g; Fiber 4g; Sugar 12.9g; Protein 8g

Maple Pumpkin Custard

Prep time: 20 minutes| **Cook time:** 1½–2 hours| **Serves:** 4 to 6

2½ cups cooked, peeled, and pureed or canned pumpkin or winter squash
2 tablespoons blackstrap molasses
3 tablespoons maple syrup
¼ cup half-and-half
3 eggs
1 teaspoon cinnamon
½ teaspoon ground ginger
½ teaspoon ground nutmeg
¼ teaspoon ground cloves
¼ teaspoon salt

Puree the quash, molasses, maple syrup, half and half, 3 eggs, cinnamon, ground ginger, nutmeg, cloves, and salt in a blender until smooth.
Pour into a slow cooker that has been oiled.
Cook on high for 1 ½–2 hours, or until the center is set and the sides are barely browning.
Serve warm as a morning side dish with toast or muffins, or in scoops over hot cereal or baked oatmeal.

Per Serving: Calories 515; Fat 35g; Sodium 348mg; Carbs 34g; Fiber 5.5g; Sugar 15g; Protein 24g

Blueberry-Flaxseed Smoothie

Prep time: 15 minutes| **Cook time:** 5 minutes| **Serves:** 8

¼ cup gluten-free rolled oats
2 teaspoons flaxseed
1 frozen ripe banana, sliced
2 cups blueberries, fresh or frozen
¾ cup unsweetened vanilla almond milk
½ cup fat-free plain Greek yogurt
2 teaspoons maple syrup or to taste
¼ teaspoon nutmeg
½ teaspoon cinnamon
½ teaspoon pure vanilla extract

Add oats, flaxseed, banana, blueberries, almond milk, yogurt, maple syrup, nutmeg, cinnamon, and vanilla extract to a blender and process until smooth.
Divide between 2 ball glasses and enjoy!

Per Serving: Calories 125; Fat 1.8g; Sodium 35mg; Carbs 27g; Fiber 2.3g; Sugar 22g; Protein 3g

Almond Oat Groats

Prep time: 5 minutes| **Cook time:** 8 to 10 hours| **Serves:** 6

1½ cups gluten-free oat groats
4 cups water
2 cups almond milk
1 to 2 cinnamon sticks
⅓ cup maple syrup
½ to 1 cup dried apples
2 scoops gluten-free vanilla-flavored protein powder, optional

In a slow cooker, add the groats, water, milk, cinnamon, maple syrup, apples, and the protein powder, if used.
Cook for 8–10 hours on low.
Take out the cinnamon sticks and serve while still hot.

Per Serving: Calories 221; Fat 5g; Sodium 151mg; Carbs 38g; Fiber 6g; Sugar 19.7g; Protein 15g

Mango, Banana, and Pineapple Smoothie

Prep time: 10 minutes| **Cook time:** 5 minutes| **Serves:** 4

6 ounces plain non-fat Greek yogurt
½ cup fresh or frozen mango chunks
½ cup fresh pineapple chunks
1 frozen banana, chopped
2 tablespoons ground flaxseed

Combine all ingredients in a blender until smooth.

Per Serving: Calories 123; Fat 2.5g; Sodium 18mg; Carbs 21.5g; Fiber 3g; Sugar 16g; Protein 5.4g

Perfect Pina Colada Smoothie

Prep time: 10 minutes| **Cook time:** 5 minutes| **Serves:** 5

1 orange, peeled
⅓ cup coconut milk
1 scoop whey protein powder
1 banana
1 cup pineapple chunks

In a blender or food processor, combine peeled orange, whey protein powder, banana, and pineapple chunks, and blend until the mixture reaches your desired consistency.

Per Serving: Calories 106; Fat 0.7g; Sodium 29mg; Carbs 22g; Fiber 2g; Sugar 16.5g; Protein 5g

Peanut Butter Blueberry Smoothie

Prep time: 10 minutes| **Cook time:** 5 minutes| **Serves:** 3

1 cup frozen blueberries
¾ cup milk, or more to taste
2 tablespoons vanilla protein powder
2 tablespoons peanut butter, or more to taste

Combine blueberries, milk, protein powder, and peanut butter in a blender, blend until smooth.

Per Serving: Calories 123; Fat 5.5g; Sodium 209mg; Carbs 13g; Fiber 2g; Sugar 9.8g; Protein 6g

Apple Granola with Sunflower Seeds

Prep time: 20 minutes| **Cook time:** 1½–2 hours| **Serves:** 12

9 cups unpeeled, sliced apples
1½ teaspoons cinnamon
1½ cups dry rolled oats
1½ cups wheat germ
1½ cups whole wheat flour
1½ cups sunflower seeds
1⅓ cups water
¾ cup honey

Prepare the slow cooker crock and grease the interior with cooking spray.
Slice the apples in your food processor. In a slow cooker, place the slices.
Sprinkle apple slices with cinnamon, then carefully whisk everything together.
Combine dry oats, wheat germ, whole wheat flour, and sunflower seeds in a large mixing dish.
Combine the dry ingredients thoroughly and then add the water and honey. Mix thoroughly with a firm spoon or your clean hands until all wet components are damp.
Pour the sauce over the apples.
Leave the lid open with a chopstick or wooden spoon handle to allow steam to escape. Turn the lid sideways if you're using an oval cooker.
Cook for 1 hour on high, stirring occasionally from the bottom and around the edges approximately every 20 minutes (Don't forget to set a timer!)
Reduce the heat to low. Continue baking for another 1–2 hours, stirring every 20 minutes or so.
When the granola starts to brown and appears dry, it's done.
Spread the granola out on parchment paper or a big baking sheet to cool and crisp up.
If you prefer clumps, there's no need to stir the granola any further as it cools. Otherwise, when the granola cools, break it up with a spoon or your hands.
Place in an airtight jar once entirely cool.

Per Serving: Calories 411; Fat 12.1g; Sodium 10mg; Carbs 72g; Fiber 9g; Sugar 41g; Protein 10.6g

Chapter 2 Vegan and Vegetarian Recipes

Instant Pot Butternut Squash

Prep time: 10 minutes| **Cook time:** 25 minutes| **Serves:** 3

1 cup water
1 whole butternut squash, less than 8 inches in length

In a 6-quart or 8-quart pressure cooker, place a trivet inside the base.
Then add the water and put the butternut squash on the trivet.
Lock the lid and adjust the valve to the "sealing" position.
Cook the butternut squash in the pressure cooker on high pressure for about 25 minutes.
Then release the pressure for about 5 to 10 minutes.
Then carefully remove the lid and transfer the squash to a cutting board with tongs.
Trim the top and end of the squash and cut it in half from top to bottom.
Scoop out the squash with a spoon. Discard the seeds. Use your spoon to scoop the squash into a serving bowl.
Serve immediately or store the cooked squash in a bowl with an air-tight lid in the refrigerator for up to 4 days.

Per Serving: Calories 22; Fat 0g; Sodium 4mg; Carbs 6g; Fiber 1g; Sugar 1g; Protein 0.5g

Turmeric Coconut Rice

Prep time: 5 minutes| **Cook time:** 6 minutes| **Serves:** 4

1 cup white basmati rice, rinsed and drained
1 cup water
2 tablespoons raisins
¼ teaspoon ground turmeric
2 tablespoons coconut butter
1 cinnamon stick

Combine the rice, water, raisins, turmeric, coconut butter, and cinnamon stick in your instant pot. Stir to combine.
Lock the lid and then let it cook on high pressure for 6 minutes.
When the cooking time is complete, let the pressure come down naturally for about 5 minutes. Then quick-release any remaining pressure.
Discard the cinnamon stick with tongs carefully. Stir the rice and serve immediately.

Per Serving: Calories 226; Fat 6g; Sodium 50mg; Carbs 39g; Fiber 2g; Sugar 0.2g; Protein 3g

Lemony Spinach and White Beans

Prep time: 15 minutes| **Cook time:** 10 minutes| **Serves:** 2

1 tablespoon olive oil
4 small plum tomatoes, halved lengthwise
10 ounces frozen spinach, defrosted and squeezed of excess water
2 garlic cloves, thinly sliced
2 tablespoons water
¼ teaspoon freshly ground black pepper
1 can white beans, drained
Juice of 1 lemon

Add oil in a large skillet and heat it up over medium-high heat. Put the tomatoes cut-side down, and cook within 3 to 5 minutes; turn and cook within 1 minute more. Transfer to a plate. Reduce heat to medium and add the spinach, garlic, water, and pepper to the skillet. Cook, tossing until the spinach is heated through, 2 to 3 minutes.
Return the tomatoes to the skillet, put the white beans and lemon juice, and toss until heated through 1 to 2 minutes.

Per Serving: Calories 222; Fat 8g; Sodium 126mg; Carbs 36g; Fiber 8g; Sugar 23g; Protein 7g

Scrambled Tofu

Prep time: 15 minutes| **Cook time:** 15 minutes| **Serves:** 1

½ tablespoon olive oil
½ red onion, chopped
2 cups chopped spinach
8 ounces firm tofu, drained well
1 teaspoon ground cumin
½ teaspoon garlic powder
Optional for serving: sliced avocado or sliced tomatoes

Heat up olive oil in a medium skillet over medium heat. Put the onion and cook within 5 minutes. Add the spinach and cover to steam for 2 minutes.
Using a spatula, move the veggies to one side of the pan. Crumble the tofu into the open area in the pan, breaking it up with a fork. Add the cumin and garlic to the crumbled tofu and mix well. Sauté for 5 to 7 minutes until the tofu is slightly browned.
Serve immediately with whole-grain bread, fruit, or beans. Top with optional sliced avocado and tomato, if using.

Per Serving: Calories 315; Fat 21g; Sodium 72mg; Carbs 14g; Fiber 3.5g; Sugar 3.8g; Protein 25.4g

Garlic Lentil and Carrot Soup

Prep time: 15 minutes| **Cook time:** 30 minutes| **Serves:** 4

1 tablespoon olive oil
2 carrots, peeled and chopped
2 celery stalks, diced
1 onion, chopped
1 teaspoon dried thyme
½ teaspoon garlic powder
1 teaspoon freshly ground black pepper
1 (28-ounce) can no-salt diced tomatoes, drained
1 cup dry lentils
5 cups water
Pinch salt

Heat up oil in a large Dutch oven or pot over medium heat. Once the oil is simmering, add the carrot, celery, and onion. Cook, often stirring, within 5 minutes.
Add the thyme, garlic powder, and black pepper. Cook within 30 seconds. Pour in the drained diced tomatoes and cook for a few more minutes, often stirring to enhance their flavor.
Put the lentils, water, and a pinch of salt. Raise the heat and bring to a boil, then partially cover the pot and reduce heat to maintain a gentle simmer.
Cook within 30 minutes or until lentils are tender but still hold their shape. Ladle into serving bowls and serve with a fresh green salad and whole-grain bread.

Per Serving: Calories 107; Fat 4g; Sodium 535mg; Carbs 17g; Fiber 6g; Sugar 7.44g; Protein 4g

Avocado, Beans, and Pepper Salad

Prep time: 6 minutes| **Cook time:** 0 minutes| **Serves:** 4

1 can pinto beans, drained
2 bell peppers, cored and chopped
1 cup corn kernels
Pinch salt
1 teaspoon freshly ground black pepper
Juice of 2 limes
1 tablespoon olive oil
1 avocado, chopped

Mix beans, peppers, corn, salt, and pepper in a large bowl. Press fresh lime juice, then mix in olive oil.
Let the salad stand in the fridge within 30 minutes. Add avocado just before serving.

Per Serving: Calories 234; Fat 12g; Sodium 538mg; Carbs 29g; Fiber 8.7g; Sugar 3g; Protein 7g

Dijon Macaroni and Cheese

Prep time: 15 minutes| **Cook time:** 20 minutes| **Serves:** 2

1 cup whole-wheat ziti macaroni
2 cups peeled and cubed butternut squash
1 cup non-fat or low-fat milk, divided
Pinch freshly ground black pepper
1 teaspoon Dijon mustard
1 tablespoon olive oil
¼ cup shredded low-fat cheddar cheese

Cook the pasta al dente. Put the butternut squash plus ½ cup milk in a medium saucepan and place over medium-high heat. Season with black pepper. Bring it to a simmer. Lower the heat, then cook until fork-tender, 8 to 10 minutes.
To a blender, add squash and Dijon mustard. Purée until smooth.
Meanwhile, add olive oil in a large sauté pan and heat it over medium heat. Add the squash purée and the remaining ½ cup of milk. Simmer within 5 minutes. Add the cheese and stir to combine.
Add the pasta to the sauté pan and stir to combine. Serve immediately.

Per Serving: Calories 358; Fat 13g; Sodium 224mg; Carbs 50g; Fiber 5.5g; Sugar 17.7g; Protein 13.6g

Parmesan Pasta with Peas and Tomatoes

Prep time: 15 minutes| **Cook time:** 15 minutes| **Serves:** 2

½ cup whole-grain pasta of choice
8 cups water, plus ¼ for finishing
1 cup frozen peas
1 tablespoon olive oil
1 cup cherry tomatoes, halved
¼ teaspoon freshly ground black pepper
1 teaspoon dried basil
¼ cup grated Parmesan cheese (low-sodium)

Cook the pasta al dente. Add the water to the same pot you used to cook the pasta, and when it's boiling, add the peas. Cook within 5 minutes. Drain and set aside.
Add 1 tablespoon of olive oil in a large skillet and heat it over medium heat. Add the cherry tomatoes, put a lid on the skillet and let the tomatoes soften for about 5 minutes, stirring a few times.
Season with black pepper and basil. Toss in the pasta, peas, and ¼ cup of water, stir and remove from the heat. Serve topped with Parmesan.

Per Serving: Calories 182; Fat 11g; Sodium 354mg; Carbs 12.8g; Fiber 3.8g; Sugar 2g; Protein 8.7g

Fried Rice with Awesome Sauce

Prep time: 15 minutes| **Cook time:** 10 minutes| **Serves:** 4

For the Sauce:
⅓ cup garlic vinegar
1 ½ tablespoons dark molasses
1 teaspoon onion powder

For the Fried Rice:
1 teaspoon olive oil
2 lightly beaten whole eggs + 4 egg whites
1 cup frozen mixed vegetables
1 cup frozen edamame
2 cups cooked brown rice

Prepare the sauce by combining the garlic vinegar, molasses, and onion powder in a glass jar. Shake well.

In a large wok, heat up the olive oil over medium-high heat. Add eggs and egg whites, and let cook until the eggs set, for about 1 minute.

Break up eggs with a spatula or spoon into small pieces. Add frozen mixed vegetables and frozen edamame. Cook for 4 minutes, stirring frequently.

Add the brown rice and sauce to the vegetable-and-egg mixture. Cook for 5 minutes or until heated through. Serve immediately.

Per Serving: Calories 272; Fat 6.3g; Sodium 113mg; Carbs 39g; Fiber 6g; Sugar 8.6g; Protein 14.5g

Stuffed Avocado

Prep time: 15 minutes| **Cook time:** 15 minutes| **Serves:** 4

2 avocados
Juice of 2 limes
1 teaspoon freshly ground black pepper
4 eggs
2 (8-inch) whole-wheat or corn tortillas, warmed
Optional for serving: halved cherry tomatoes and chopped cilantro

Adjust the oven rack to the middle position and preheat the oven to 450°F/205°C. Scrape out the center of a halved avocado using a spoon of about 1 ½ tablespoon.

Press lime juice over the avocados and season with black pepper to taste, and then place it on a baking sheet. Crack an egg into the avocado.

Bake within 10 to 15 minutes. Remove from oven and garnish with optional cilantro and cherry tomatoes and serve with warm tortillas.

Per Serving: Calories 361; Fat 26.4g; Sodium 215mg; Carbs 21g; Fiber 9g; Sugar 2g; Protein 13g

Spinach and Beans with Rice

Prep time: 15 minutes| **Cook time:** 45 minutes| **Serves:** 2

½ cup dry brown rice
1 cup water, plus ¼ cup
1 can red beans, drained
1 tablespoon ground cumin
Juice of 1 lime
4 handfuls of fresh spinach
Optional toppings: avocado, chopped tomatoes, Greek yogurt, onions

Mix rice plus water in a pot and bring to a boil. Cover and reduce heat to a low simmer. Cook within 30 to 40 minutes or according to package directions.
Meanwhile, add the beans, ¼ cup of water, cumin, and lime juice to a medium skillet. Simmer within 5 to 7 minutes.
Once the liquid is mostly gone, remove it from the heat and add spinach. Cover and let spinach wilt slightly for 2 to 3 minutes. Mix in with the beans. Serve beans with rice. Add toppings if using.

Per Serving: Calories 362; Fat 3.6g; Sodium 351mg; Carbs 69g; Fiber 10g; Sugar 6g; Protein 16g

Black Beans and Tomato Soup

Prep time: 15 minutes| **Cook time:** 20 minutes| **Serves:** 4

1 yellow onion
1 tablespoon olive oil
2 cans black beans, drained
1 cup diced fresh tomatoes
5 cups low-sodium vegetable broth
¼ teaspoon freshly ground black pepper
¼ cup chopped fresh cilantro

Cook or sauté the onion in the olive oil within 4 to 5 minutes in a large saucepan over medium heat.
Put the black beans, tomatoes, vegetable broth, and black pepper. Boil, then adjust heat to simmer within 15 minutes.
Remove, then working in batches, ladle the soup into a blender, and process until somewhat smooth.
Return it to the pot, add cilantro, and heat until warmed through. Serve immediately.

Per Serving: Calories 310; Fat 7g; Sodium 1250mg; Carbs 54g; Fiber 11g; Sugar 21g; Protein 11g

Awesome Brown Rice

Prep time: 5 minutes| **Cook time:** 10 minutes| **Serves:** 4

1 cup low-sodium vegetable broth
½ tablespoon olive oil
1 garlic clove, minced
1 scallion, thinly sliced
1 tablespoon minced onion flakes
1 cup instant brown rice
⅛ teaspoon freshly ground black pepper

Mix the vegetable broth, olive oil, garlic, scallion, and minced onion flakes in a saucepan and boil.
Put rice, then boil it again, adjust the heat and simmer within 10 minutes.
Remove and let stand within 5 minutes.
Use a fork to fluff and season with black pepper.
Serve over instant brown rice.

Per Serving: Calories 117; Fat 2.7g; Sodium 246mg; Carbs 20.4g; Fiber 2.4g; Sugar 3.5g; Protein 2.8g

Instant Pot Rice with Olives

Prep time: 10 minutes| **Cook time:** 15 minutes| **Serves:** 4

1 teaspoon avocado oil or olive oil
1 small red onion, chopped, about ¾ cup
1 ¼ cups reduced-sodium chicken or vegetable broth
1 tablespoon tomato paste
¼ teaspoon chili powder
1 cup white rice, rinsed
¼ cup pitted black olives
½ teaspoon salt

Turn on the Sauté function on your 6-quart Instant Pot. Add the avocado or olive oil and let it heat up for about 2 minutes.
Add the chopped onion and let it sauté for about 3 minutes, stirring occasionally.
Cancel the Sauté function and add the broth, tomato paste, chili powder, and rice, and stir to combine.
Lock the lid. Adjust the setting to 6 minutes on high pressure.
When the cooking time is up, let the pressure come down naturally for 10 minutes. Remove the lid. Then stir in the olives and salt.
Serve hot or store in a tightly-sealed container in the refrigerator for up to 5 days.

Per Serving: Calories 250; Fat 4.4g; Sodium 519mg; Carbs 46.6g; Fiber 2.8g; Sugar 3.5g; Protein 5.5g

Garlic Cauliflower

Prep time: 10 minutes| **Cook time:** 10 minutes| **Serves:** 4

16 cups water (enough to cover cauliflower)
1 head cauliflower (about 3 pounds), trimmed and cut into florets
4 garlic cloves
1 tablespoon olive oil
¼ teaspoon salt
⅛ teaspoon freshly ground black pepper
2 teaspoons dried parsley

Boil a large pot of water, then the cauliflower and garlic. Cook within 10 minutes, then strain. Move it back to the hot pan, and let it stand within 2 to 3 minutes with the lid on.
Put the cauliflower plus garlic in a food processor or blender. Add the olive oil, salt, pepper, and purée until smooth. Taste and adjust the salt and pepper.
Remove, then put the parsley, and mix until combined. Garnish with additional olive oil, if desired. Serve immediately.

Per Serving: Calories 51; Fat 3.6g; Sodium 185mg; Carbs 4g; Fiber 1g; Sugar 1g; Protein 1.5g

Balsamic Zucchini Kebabs

Prep time: 15 minutes| **Cook time:** 6 minutes| **Serves:** 4

2 tablespoons balsamic vinegar
1 tablespoon olive oil
1 teaspoon dried parsley
2 tablespoons water
2 sweet peppers
2 red onions, peeled
2 zucchinis, trimmed

Cut the sweet peppers and onions into squares of medium size. Next, shave the zucchini. Thread each vegetable onto a skewer. Next, combine olive oil, dried parsley, water, and balsamic vinegar in the shallow bowl.
Sprinkle the vegetable skewers with the olive oil mixture and place them on a grill preheated to 390°F/200°C. The kebabs should be cooked for 3 minutes per side, or until the vegetables are golden brown.

Per Serving: Calories 86; Fat 3.6g; Sodium 7mg; Carbs 12.6g; Fiber 2g; Sugar 3.5g; Protein 1.7g

Carrot and Peas Salad

Prep time: 15 minutes| **Cook time:** 6 minutes| **Serves:** 2

1 tablespoon olive oil
3 cups purple cabbage, chopped
5 cups baby spinach
1 cup shredded carrots
1 can black-eyed peas, drained
Juice of ½ lemon
Pinch salt
1 teaspoon freshly ground black pepper

In a medium pan, add the oil and cabbage and sauté for 1 to 2 minutes on medium heat.
Add in your spinach, and cover for 3 to 4 minutes on medium heat, until greens are wilted. Remove from the heat and add to a large bowl.
Add in the carrots, black-eyed peas, and a splash of lemon juice. Season with salt and pepper, if desired. Toss and serve.

Per Serving: Calories 294; Fat 15g; Sodium 1043mg; Carbs 39g; Fiber 13g; Sugar 17g; Protein 9.6g

Avocado and Cucumber Soup

Prep time: 15 minutes| **Cook time:** 30 minutes| **Serves:** 4

2 English cucumbers, peeled and diced, plus ¼ cup reserved for garnish
1 avocado, peeled, pitted, and chopped, plus ¼ cup reserved for garnish
1 ½ cups non-fat or low-fat plain Greek yogurt
½ cup cold water
⅓ cup loosely packed dill, plus sprigs for garnish
1 tablespoon freshly squeezed lemon juice
¼ teaspoon freshly ground black pepper
¼ teaspoon salt
1 garlic clove

Purée all the ingredients excluding the garnish ingredients in a blender until smooth. If you prefer a thinner soup, add more water until you reach the desired consistency.
Divide soup among 4 bowls. Cover with plastic wrap and refrigerate within 30 minutes. Garnish with cucumber, avocado, and dill sprigs, if desired.

Per Serving: Calories 177; Fat 9g; Sodium 135mg; Carbs 18g; Fiber 6g; Sugar 7.7g; Protein 10.5g

Carrot and Pepper with Cottage

Prep time: 15 minutes| **Cook time:** 30 minutes| **Serves:** 6

1 cup carrot, diced
½ cup bell pepper, diced
1 cup spinach, chopped
1 tablespoon olive oil
1 teaspoon chili powder
1 cup tomatoes, chopped
2 ounces low-fat cottage cheese
1 eggplant, sliced
1 cup low-sodium vegetable broth

Carrot, bell pepper, and spinach should be placed in the saucepan. Add olive oil and chili powder to the vegetables and mix thoroughly. Prepare them for 5 minutes.
Make the sliced eggplant layer in the casserole mold and top it with a vegetable mixture. Add tomatoes, vegetable stock, and cottage cheese.
Bake the lasagna for 30 minutes at 375°F/190°C.

Per Serving: Calories 96; Fat 4.8g; Sodium 130mg; Carbs 10.5g; Fiber 4g; Sugar 6g; Protein 4.6g

Garlic Broccoli

Prep time: 2 minutes| **Cook time:** 4 minutes| **Serves:** 4

1 cup water
4 cups broccoli florets
1 teaspoon olive oil
1 tablespoon minced garlic
1 teaspoon lemon zest
Pinch salt
1 teaspoon freshly ground black pepper

Put the broccoli in the boiling water in a small saucepan and cook for 2 to 3 minutes. The broccoli should retain its bright-green color. Drain the water from the broccoli.
Put the olive oil in a small sauté pan over medium-high heat.
Add the garlic and sauté for 30 seconds.
Put the broccoli, lemon zest, salt, plus pepper. Combine well and serve.

Per Serving: Calories 24; Fat 1.4g; Sodium 209mg; Carbs 2.3g; Fiber 1.3g; Sugar 0.2g; Protein 1.5g

Rosemary-Chickpea Omelet

Prep time: 15 minutes| **Cook time:** 15 minutes| **Serves:** 2

½ tablespoon olive oil
4 eggs
¼ cup grated Parmesan cheese
1 (15-ounce) can chickpeas, drained and rinsed
2 cups packed baby spinach
1 cup button mushrooms, chopped
2 sprigs rosemary, leaves picked (or 2 teaspoons dried rosemary)
Pinch salt
1 teaspoon freshly ground black pepper

Warm oven to 400°F/205°C and put a baking tray on the middle shelf.
Prepare an 8-inch springform pan, line it with baking paper, and grease generously with olive oil. If you don't have a springform pan, grease an oven-safe skillet (or cast-iron skillet) with olive oil.
Lightly whisk the eggs and Parmesan. Place chickpeas in the prepared pan. Layer the spinach and mushrooms on top of the beans. Pour the egg mixture on top and scatter the rosemary. Season to taste with salt and pepper.
Place the pan on the preheated tray and bake until golden and puffy and the center feels firm and springy for about 15 minutes. Remove from the oven, slice, and serve immediately.

Per Serving: Calories 408; Fat 19g; Sodium 1228mg; Carbs 35.6g; Fiber 10g; Sugar 6.5g; Protein 26g

Savory Baked Potatoes

Prep time: 5 minutes| **Cook time:** 20 minutes| **Serves:** 8

1 cup water
4 to 8 large Russet potatoes, scrubbed and patted dry

Place the trivet inside of a 6-quart or 8-quart Instant Pot.
Pour in the water and add the potatoes on top. Lock on the lid and let it cook for 20 minutes on high pressure.
Once the cooking time is complete, naturally release the pressure for 10 minutes. Then release the remaining pressure and remove the lid.
Use tongs to remove the potatoes. Serve warm.

Per Serving: Calories 292; Fat 0.3g; Sodium 19mg; Carbs 66.7g; Fiber 4.8g; Sugar 2.3g; Protein 8g

Zuccchini and Beans Burrito

Prep time: 15 minutes| **Cook time:** 15 minutes| **Serves:** 4

½ tablespoon olive oil
2 red or green bell peppers, chopped
1 zucchini or summer squash, diced
½ teaspoon chili powder
1 teaspoon cumin
Freshly ground black pepper
1 can black beans, drained and rinsed
1 cup cherry tomatoes, halved
4 (8-inch) whole-wheat tortillas
Optional for serving: spinach, sliced avocado, chopped scallions, or hot sauce

Heat up oil in a large sauté pan over medium heat. Add the bell peppers and sauté until crisp-tender, about 4 minutes.
Add the zucchini, chili powder, cumin, and black pepper to taste, and continue to sauté until the vegetables are tender about 5 minutes.
Add the black beans and cherry tomatoes and cook within 5 minutes. Divide between 4 burritos and serve topped with optional ingredients as desired. Enjoy immediately.

Per Serving: Calories 428; Fat 7g; Sodium 234mg; Carbs 73g; Fiber 17g; Sugar 9.6g; Protein 21g

Chapter 3 Salad and Sides Recipes

Sautéed Zucchini

Prep time: 10 minutes | **Cook time:** 10 minutes | **Serves:** 4

1¼-pound chopped zucchini (2 medium)
1 tablespoon butter
1 tablespoon minced garlic (3 cloves)
1 scallion, thinly sliced
1 to 2 teaspoons fresh lemon juice or red wine vinegar, optional
¼ cup of freshly grated parmesan or pecorino cheese, optional
Salt and new ground black pepper

Slice the zucchini into rounds, half-moons, or bite-size chunks.
Melt the butter in a large pan over medium-high heat; add the zucchini to the pan, and sauté for 3 to 5 minutes until browned in spots and soft.
Turn off the heat, add the scallions, lemon juice, cheese (optional), salt, and black pepper to the pan, toss well.
Serve the food to the plate, and enjoy.

Per Serving: Calories 91; Fat 5.23g; Sodium 119mg; Carbs 7.33g; Fiber 1.9g; Sugar 0.69g; Protein 6.08g

Healthy Apple, Spinach & Eggs Salad

Prep time: 10 minutes | **Cook time:** 0 | **Serves:** 2

4 quartered hard boiled eggs
2 granny Smith apples, chopped
2 cups spinach
½ cup ground hazelnuts
1 tablespoon olive oil or avocado oil
1 tablespoon fresh lemon juice
Pinch of black pepper
Pinch of sea salt

Mix all ingredients except for the ground hazelnuts in the serving bowl.
Top the salad with the ground hazelnuts, and enjoy.

Per Serving: Calories 508; Fat 34.16g; Sodium 289mg; Carbs 33.23g; Fiber 9g; Sugar 20.07g; Protein 19.72g

Chickpeas, Onion, Tomato & Parsley in a Jar

Prep time: 10 minutes | **Cook time:** 0 | **Serves:** 2

1 cup cooked chickpeas
½ cup chopped tomatoes
½ of a small onion, chopped
1 tablespoon chia seeds
1 tablespoon chopped parsley
Dressing:
1 tablespoon olive oil
1 tablespoon of Chlorella.
1 tablespoon fresh lemon juice
Pinch of sea salt

Mix all the dressing ingredients in the jar.
Then add the tomatoes, chickpeas, onions, chia seeds and parsley to the jar in order. Enjoy.

Per Serving: Calories 231; Fat 10.31g; Sodium 88mg; Carbs 28.01g; Fiber 8.5g; Sugar 5.87g; Protein 8.57g

Arugula, Carrot, Corn & Spinach in a Jar

Prep time: 10 minutes | **Cook time:** 0 | **Serves:** 2

1 cup corn
1 cup tomatoes
½ cup of julienned carrot
½ cup spinach
Dressing:
1 tablespoon olive oil
2 tablespoons Greek yogurt
1 tablespoon fresh lemon juice
Pinch of sea salt

Mix the olive oil, yogurt, lemon juice, and sea salt in the bottom of the jar.
Then add the tomatoes, corn, carrots, and arugula to the jar in order.

Per Serving: Calories 201; Fat 7.7g; Sodium 470mg; Carbs 32.96g; Fiber 4.3g; Sugar 9.42g; Protein 5.3g

Shrimp, Cucumber & Arugula

Prep time: 10 minutes | **Cook time:** 0 | **Serves:** 2

1 cup cooked shrimp
½ cup of cucumber
1 cup of arugula
Dressing:
1 tablespoon olive oil
1 tablespoon fresh lemon juice
Pinch of sea salt

Mix the olive oil, lemon juice, and sea salt in the bottom of the jar.
Then add the cucumber, shrimp, and arugula to the jar in order.

Per Serving: Calories 135; Fat 7.8g; Sodium 638mg; Carbs 2.18g; Fiber 0.6g; Sugar 1.22g; Protein 13.7g

Tomato, Cucumber, Pumpkin & Dandelion

Prep time: 10 minutes | **Cook time:** 0 | **Serves:** 2

½ cup cooked, cubed pumpkin
½ cup tomatoes
½ cup of sliced cucumber
½ cup dandelion leaves
Dressing:
1 tablespoon olive oil
1 tablespoon of Chlorella
1 tablespoon fresh lemon juice
Pinch of sea salt

Mix the olive oil, Chlorella, lemon juice, and sea salt in the bottom of the jar.
Add the tomatoes, cucumbers, pumpkin and dandelion leaves to the jar in order.

Per Serving: Calories 244; Fat 21.41g; Sodium 166mg; Carbs 7.62g; Fiber 2.9g; Sugar 1.67g; Protein 9.54g

Carrot, Peppers, Cucumber & Cabbage

Prep time: 10 minutes | **Cook time:** 0 | **Serves:** 2

½ cup chopped cucumber
½ cup chopped carrots
½ cup of shredded red cabbage
½ cup of red peppers
1 cup lettuce
Dressing:
1 tablespoon olive oil
1 tablespoon fresh lemon juice
Pinch of sea salt

Mix the olive oil, lemon juice, and sea salt in the bottom of the jar.
Put the cucumbers, peppers, cabbage, carrots and lettuce to the jar in order.

Per Serving: Calories 94; Fat 7.05g; Sodium 106mg; Carbs 7.44g; Fiber 2.3g; Sugar 3.98g; Protein 1.38g

Tomato, Cucumber, Carrot & Parsley Salad

Prep time: 10 minutes | **Cook time:** 0 | **Serves:** 2

½ cup red tomatoes
½ cup yellow tomatoes
½ cup of sliced carrot
1 tablespoon of chopped parsley
Dressing:
1 tablespoon olive oil
2 tablespoons Greek yogurt
1 tablespoon fresh lemon juice
Pinch of sea salt

Mix the olive oil, yogurt, lemon juice, and sea salt in the bottom of the jar.
Put the yellow tomato, carrots, red tomato and parsley over the dressing in order.

Per Serving: Calories 86; Fat 7.49g; Sodium 100mg; Carbs 4.46g; Fiber 0.9g; Sugar 1.94g; Protein 1.47g

Apple Pepper Coleslaw

Prep time: 10 minutes | **Cook time:** 0 | **Serves:** 1-2

1 cup chopped cabbage (various color)
1 tart apple chopped
1 celery, chopped
1 red pepper chopped
5 teaspoons olive oil or avocado oil
juice of 1 lemon
2 teaspoons lucuma powder (optional)
Dash sea salt

Combine the cabbage, apple, celery, and pepper together in a large bowl.
Mix the remaining ingredients in a smaller bowl.
Mix them together, drizzle over coleslaw, and toss to coat. Enjoy.

Per Serving: Calories 135; Fat 5.33g; Sodium 232mg; Carbs 22.88g; Fiber 4.7g; Sugar 13.79g; Protein 2.02g

Chicken & Roasted Veggies Salad

Prep time: 10 minutes | **Cook time:** 0 | **Serves:** 2

1 cup sliced grilled chicken
½ cup tomato
½ cup grilled veggies
1 cup arugula
½ cup chopped red peppers
1 tablespoon olive oil or avocado oil
1 tablespoon fresh lemon juice
Pinch of black pepper
Pinch of sea salt

Add all the ingredients to a serving bowl.
Mix them well, and you can enjoy.

Per Serving: Calories 308; Fat 26.19g; Sodium 183mg; Carbs 5.1g; Fiber 1.8g; Sugar 3.03g; Protein 13.27g

Broccoli Seafood Salad

Prep time: 10 minutes | **Cook time:** 0 | **Serves:** 2

1 cup cooked quinoa mixed with 1 tablespoon ground flax seeds
1 cup stir fried broccoli
½ cup green peas
1 cup stir fried shrimp and scallops
1 tablespoon olive oil
1 tablespoon fresh lemon juice
Pinch of black pepper
Pinch of sea salt

Add all the ingredients to a serving bowl.
Mix them well, and you can enjoy.

Per Serving: Calories 254; Fat 10.27g; Sodium 216mg; Carbs 33.25g; Fiber 6.9g; Sugar 2.6g; Protein 10.18g

Tuna, Veggies & Eggs Salad

Prep time: 10 minutes | **Cook time:** 0 | **Serves:** 2

1 cup tuna chunks
½ cup chopped tomato
2 halved eggs
1 cup arugula
½ cup sliced yellow peppers
1 tablespoon olive oil
1 tablespoon fresh lemon juice
Pinch of black pepper
Pinch of sea salt

Add all the ingredients to a serving bowl.
Mix them well, and you can enjoy.

Per Serving: Calories 212; Fat 11.93g; Sodium 336mg; Carbs 5.63g; Fiber 1.1g; Sugar 1.54g; Protein 21.58g

Easy Avocado, Tomato, Arugula Salad

Prep time: 10 minutes | **Cook time:** 0 | **Serves:** 2

1 cup orange tomatoes
½ cup chopped avocado
½ cup arugula radish
1 cup red tomatoes
1 tablespoon olive oil
1 tablespoon fresh lemon juice
Pinch of black pepper
Pinch of sea salt

Add all the ingredients to a serving bowl.
Mix them well, and you can enjoy.

Per Serving: Calories 197; Fat 12.6g; Sodium 88mg; Carbs 21.21g; Fiber 3.9g; Sugar 12.85g; Protein 2.41g

Vegetable Chicken Salad

Prep time: 10 minutes | **Cook time:** 0 | **Serves:** 2

1 cup grilled chicken
½ cup chopped cucumber
½ cup chopped tomato
1 cup cooked spinach
1 tablespoon olive oil or avocado oil
1 tablespoon fresh lemon juice
Pinch of black pepper
Pinch of sea salt

Add all the ingredients to a serving bowl.
Mix them well, and you can enjoy.

Per Serving: Calories 314; Fat 26.16g; Sodium 239mg; Carbs 6.03g; Fiber 2.9g; Sugar 1.97g; Protein 14.64g

Easy Green Pomegranate Salad

Prep time: 10 minutes | **Cook time:** 0 | **Serves:** 2

1 cup mixed greens, spinach, arugula, red leaf lettuce
1 ripe avocado, cut into ½-inch pieces
½ cup pomegranate seeds
¼ cup pecan
¼ cup blackberries
¼ cup cherry tomatoes
olive oil or avocado oil, salt, lemon juice

Mix lettuce, tomatoes, cucumber, pepper, onion, radishes, and parsley. Combine the olive oil, lemon juice, garlic, salt, pepper, and mint in a mixing bowl.
Serve and enjoy.

Per Serving: Calories 345; Fat 24.61g; Sodium 53mg; Carbs 33.51g; Fiber 12.6g; Sugar 17.93g; Protein 5.26g

Vegetable Salad in a Jar

Prep time: 10 minutes | **Cook time:** 0 | **Serves:** 2

½ cup sunflower seeds
½ cup carrots
½ cup of shredded cabbage
½ cup of tomatoes
1 cup cooked quinoa mixed with 1 tablespoon chia seeds
1 cup spinach

Dressing:
1 tablespoon olive oil
1 tablespoon fresh lemon juice
Pinch of sea salt

Combine the olive oil, lemon juice, and sea salt in a small bowl to make the dressing.
Add the dressing, carrots, cabbage, tomatoes, spinach, and quinoa mixture to the jar in order, enjoy.

Per Serving: Calories 429; Fat 29.11g; Sodium 125mg; Carbs 35.19g; Fiber 9.9g; Sugar 4.2g; Protein 11.9g

Keto Cauliflower Rice

Prep time: 10 minutes | **Cook time:** 10 minutes | **Serves:** 3

1 head of cauliflower
4 tablespoon butter
pink Himalayan salt
fresh ground black pepper, as need

Remove the cauliflower florets, and then process the florets in a food processor until they reach a rice-like consistency.
Heat the butter, and cauliflower in the nonstick pan over medium-high heat.
Season the cauliflower with salt and pepper.
Turn off the heat, transfer the food to the serving plate, and enjoy.

Per Serving: Calories 160; Fat 15.63g; Sodium 80mg; Carbs 4.89g; Fiber 2g; Sugar 1.7g; Protein 1.94g

Sautéed Spinach

Prep time: 10 minutes | **Cook time:** 10 minutes | **Serves:** 2

1 tablespoon olive oil
2 garlic cloves, peeled and smashed
1 (12-ounce) package baby spinach
¼ teaspoon salt
⅛ teaspoon freshly ground black pepper
⅛ teaspoon dried crushed red pepper
¼ cup of golden raisins
¼ cup of slivered almonds

Heat the olive oil in a big saucepan over medium-high heat.
After 30 seconds, add the garlic, spinach, and the remaining ingredients to the saucepan.
Cover the saucepan, and cook them for 3 minutes until spinach wilts, stirring regularly.
Cook for 1 to 2 minutes more, stirring in raisins and almonds.
Serve and enjoy.

Per Serving: Calories 133; Fat 7.03g; Sodium 312mg; Carbs 18.4g; Fiber 1.5g; Sugar 12.36g; Protein 1.59g

Artichoke Lamb Salad

Prep time: 10 minutes | **Cook time:** 0 | **Serves:** 2

1 cup sliced roasted lamb
1 cup roasted quartered artichoke hearts
½ cup chopped red onion
1 cup Arugula
1 tablespoon olive oil or avocado oil
1 tablespoon fresh lemon juice
Pinch of black pepper
Pinch of sea salt

Add all the ingredients to a serving bowl.
Mix them well, and then enjoy.

Per Serving: Calories 248; Fat 14.54g; Sodium 238mg; Carbs 13.65g; Fiber 7.9g; Sugar 2.45g; Protein 17.09g

Tuna, Eggs & Lettuce Salad

Prep time: 10 minutes | **Cook time:** 0 | **Serves:** 2

1 cup tuna
2 boiled eggs, sliced
1 cup chopped tomato
1 cup lettuce
1 tablespoon olive oil or avocado oil
1 tablespoon fresh lemon juice
Pinch of black pepper
Pinch of sea salt

Mix all the ingredients in a large bowl.
Apportion the salad between the plates, and enjoy.

Per Serving: Calories 190; Fat 9.27g; Sodium 395mg; Carbs 4.63g; Fiber 1.2g; Sugar 2.97g; Protein 22.35g

Creamy Cauliflower

Prep time: 10 minutes | **Cook time:** 10 minutes | **Serves:** 6

2-pound cauliflower florets
2 garlic cloves, peeled, whole
2 tablespoons unsalted butter
¼ cup of parmesan cheese, shredded
¼ cup of sour cream, optional
1–3 tablespoons cooking water
Salt and pepper, as need
Garnishes (optional):
Melted butter, parsley, pepper

Half the big florets.
Boil a large saucepan of water.
Add the cauliflower, and garlic to the boiling water, and simmer for 10 minutes until very soft.
Take a cup of cooking water and scoop it out.
Drain the cauliflower well, and then transfer to a food processor.
Blitz the remaining ingredients until smooth, starting with no water.
Season with salt, and pepper.
Transfer the food to a serving plate. If desired, drizzle with melted butter, garnish with parsley, and serve as a side dish with anything that goes well with mashed potatoes.

Per Serving: Calories 96; Fat 5.2g; Sodium 159mg; Carbs 9.85g; Fiber 3.2g; Sugar 3.46g; Protein 4.75g

Chapter 4 Lunch Recipes

Walnut Mushroom Gravy

Prep time: 12 minutes| **Cook time:** 15 minutes| **Serves:** 3

1 pinch cayenne pepper
1 pinch sea salt
1 cup homemade walnut milk
2 tablespoons finely chopped walnuts
¼ diced onion
½ teaspoon fresh thyme
1-½ tablespoons amaranth
2 tablespoons grapeseed oil
1 cup thinly sliced mushrooms
½ cup homemade vegetable broth

Over medium heat, add grape seed oil to a large saucepan. After this, add mushrooms and onion and add a pinch of cayenne pepper and sea salt. Allow to cook for 4 minutes.
Add amaranth and beater to coat. Allow this to cook for 90 seconds.
Afterward, gradually whisk in walnut milk and vegetable broth.
Start this with ½ cup walnut milk and increase as you move on.
Again, season with a pinch of cayenne pepper and sea salt. Over low heat, stir frequently, and cook until condensed. Add all the walnuts and stir. Serve over plant-based biscuits.

Per Serving: Calories 139; Fat 8g; Sodium 517mg; Carbs 12.8g; Fiber 2g; Sugar 9g; Protein 5.6g

Avocado, Beans, and Nuts Salad

Prep time: 15 minutes| **Cook time:** 0 minutes| **Serves:** 2

5 cups Romaine lettuce
½ cup sprouted black beans
1 cup halved cherry tomatoes
1 diced avocado
¼ cup chopped almonds
½ cup fresh cilantro
½ cup Salsa Fresca

Take a large sized bowl and add lettuce, tomatoes, beans, almonds, cilantro, avocado, Salsa Fresco. Toss everything well and mix them. Divide the salad into serving bowls and serve!

Per Serving: Calories 411; Fat 16g; Sodium 487mg; Carbs 58g; Fiber 19g; Sugar 15g; Protein 16g

Wrapped Bacon, Avocado, and Tomato with Basil-Mayo

Prep time: 5 minutes| **Cook time:** 15 minutes| **Serves:** 4

1 iceberg lettuce head
4 deli turkey slices gluten-free (I like Applegate Farms)
4 slices cooked gluten-free bacon (I like Applegate Farms)
1 finely sliced avocado
1 finely sliced Roma tomato
For the Basil-Mayo:
½ gluten-free cup mayonnaise (I prefer Hellmann's Olive Oil Mayo).
6 basil leaves, big, ripped
1 teaspoon freshly squeezed lemon juice
1 minced garlic clove salt and pepper

Basil-Mayo: Add all ingredients and pulse until smooth in a small food processor. Alternatively, mince the basil and garlic and then whisk together all ingredients. It can be completed a couple of days in advance.
Arrange two large lettuce leaves on a plate, top with 1 slice turkey, and drizzle with Basil-Mayo. Continue layering with the second piece of turkey, bacon, and a few slices of avocado and tomato.
Then add a little salt and pepper. Fold up the bottom, the sides in, and roll the burrito-style. Serve chilled after slicing in half.

Per Serving: Calories 327; Fat 28g; Sodium 504mg; Carbs 13.7g; Fiber 6g; Sugar 6.4g; Protein 8.4g

Mozzarella Lasagna Rolls

Prep time: 15 minutes| **Cook time:** 15 minutes| **Serves:** 2

½ cup lasagna noodles
½ cup vegan mozzarella, shredded
¼ cup kale
½ cup marinara sauce
salt and pepper to taste
enough water

Set Instant Pot to Sauté. Add the kale with the vegan mozzarella, pepper and salt. Stir regularly.
Add marinara sauce, water, noodles. Mix well. Stir to avoid the noodles become sticky.
Lock lid and make sure its vent is closed. Set your Instant Pot to Pressure Cook mode on High for 15 minutes. When cooking time ends, release pressure and wait for steam to stop before opening lid completely.

Per Serving: Calories 206; Fat 9g; Sodium 608mg; Carbs 18g; Fiber 3g; Sugar 6.8g; Protein 13.4g

Kale Garbanzo Burgers

Prep time: 35 minutes| **Cook time:** 55 minutes| **Serves:** 3

1 cup Garbanzo beans flour
1 teaspoon grapeseed oil
2 teaspoons oregano
2 teaspoons basil
½ teaspoon cayenne pepper
½ cup kale, diced
1 diced plum tomato
2 teaspoons onion powder
2 teaspoons sea salt
½ cup diced green peppers
½ teaspoon ginger powder
1 teaspoon dill
½ cup spring water

Mix the vegetables and seasonings in a big bowl, then add the flour. Add water and combine the other ingredients until it forms a patty. You can add more flour if the patty is too light.
Add the grape seed oil to a skillet, then let the patty boil on each side for at least 2 minutes on medium heat.
Then flip continually until each side becomes brown. Serve on Alkaline flatbread. Enjoy.

Per Serving: Calories 287; Fat 5g; Sodium 1315mg; Carbs 49g; Fiber 9g; Sugar 11g; Protein 14.6g

Lime Avocado Pasta

Prep time: 10 minutes| **Cook time:** 20 minutes| **Serves:** 4

4 cups cooked spelt pasta
1 medium diced avocado
2 cups halved cherry tomatoes
1 minced fresh basil
1 teaspoon agave syrup
1 tablespoon key lime juice
¼ cup olive oil
Pure seas salt, to taste

Place the cooked pasta in a large bowl. Add diced avocado, halved cherry tomatoes, and minced basil into the bowl. Stir all the mixture until well combined. Whisk agave syrup, olive oil, and pure sea salt and key lime juice in a separate bowl.
Pour it over the pasta and stir until well combined.

Per Serving: Calories 496; Fat 23g; Sodium 23mg; Carbs 68g; Fiber 12g; Sugar 16g; Protein 12.6g

Basil Spelt Flatbread

Prep time: 40 minutes| **Cook time:** 60 minutes| **Serves:** 6

2 teaspoons oregano
2 teaspoons basil
2 tablespoons grapeseed oil
2 teaspoons onion powder
2 cups spelt flour
¼ teaspoon cayenne pepper
1 tablespoon sea salt
¾ cup spring water

Combine the spelt flour and the seasonings until it becomes appropriately mixed. Add ¼ cup of the spring water and grape seed oil into the mixture.
Add water slowly until the mixture forms balls. Spread the flour unto a workstation, then work on the dough for at least 4 minutes before dividing the dough into 5 parts. Ensure the five parts are equal. Now roll each of the balls into 5 inches' circle.
Put the rolled flour balls on a skillet and place on medium heat. Don't grease the skillet with oil. Flip the balls at 3 minutes' intervals until it is well cooked. Then serve and enjoy.

Per Serving: Calories 217; Fat 3g; Sodium 329mg; Carbs 42g; Fiber 6.8g; Sugar 4g; Protein 9g

Garlic Spaghetti with Bolognese Sauce

Prep time: 20 minutes| **Cook time:** 20 minutes| **Serves:** 2

½ pound lean ground beef (90% lean)
1 medium carrot, shredded
1 celery rib, thinly sliced
¼ cup chopped onion
1 garlic clove, minced
1 jar (14 ounces) spaghetti sauce
½ teaspoon Italian seasoning
1 tablespoon heavy whipping cream or milk
1 tablespoon minced fresh parsley
4 ounces uncooked spaghetti

Cook the beef, carrot, celery, onion, and garlic in a large pan over medium heat until the meat is no longer pink. Bring to a boil, stirring in spaghetti sauce and Italian seasoning. Incorporate the cream and parsley. Then cook for ten minutes covered over low heat.
Meanwhile, prepare spaghetti according to the directions on the box; drain. Toss with sauce. Cook for 1-2 minutes, or until well heated. Serve right away.

Per Serving: Calories 463; Fat 18.7g; Sodium 995mg; Carbs 36g; Fiber 7.7g; Sugar 14g; Protein 37g

Mozzarella Margherita Pizza

Prep time: 10 minutes| **Cook time:** 5 minutes| **Serves:** 1

1 tablespoon phylum husk powder
¼ teaspoon salt
½ teaspoon dried oregano
1 egg (egg consumption should be minimized)
1 tablespoon avocado oil
3 tablespoons low-sugar marinara sauce
½ cup sliced vegan mozzarella cheese
1 tablespoon chopped fresh basil

Line a baking sheet with aluminum foil. Turn the oven to low broil. Combine the phylum husk powder, salt, oregano, and egg in a blender. Blend for 30 seconds. Set aside. In a sauté pan or skillet, over high heat, warm the avocado oil.
Pour the crust mixture into the pan, spreading it out into a circle. Cook the mixture until the edges are browned, then flip the crust and cook for an additional minute. Transfer the crust to the baking sheet. Spread the marinara sauce over the top and cover with the vegan mozzarella cheeses. Broil until the cheese is melted and bubbling. Top with the basil and enjoy.

Per Serving: Calories 326; Fat 27.5g; Sodium 816mg; Carbs 7.6g; Fiber 1.8g; Sugar 4.4g; Protein 12.6g

Sautéed Zucchinis and Eggplants

Prep time: 10 minutes| **Cook time:** 20 minutes| **Serves:** 4

1 tablespoon olive oil
2 zucchinis, sliced
1 eggplant, roughly cubed
2 scallions, chopped
1 tablespoon sweet paprika
juice of 1 lime
1 teaspoon fennel seeds, crushed
salt and black pepper to the taste
1 tablespoon basil, chopped

In a pan, scoop in the olive oil and then heat it up over medium heat.
Add the scallions and fennel seeds and sauté for 5 minutes.
Add zucchinis, eggplant and the other ingredients, toss, cook over medium heat for 15 minutes more, divide between plates and serve as a side dish.

Per Serving: Calories 82; Fat 4g; Sodium 7mg; Carbs 12g; Fiber 5g; Sugar 6g; Protein 2g

Macaroni and Cheese with Nuts

Prep time: 20 minutes| **Cook time:** 50 minutes| **Serves:** 8 to 10

12 ounces any alkaline pasta
¼ cup chickpea flour
1 cup raw Brazil nuts
½ teaspoon ground achiote
2 teaspoons onion powder
1 teaspoon pure sea salt
2 teaspoons grapeseed oil
1 cup homemade hempseed milk
1 cup spring water + extra for soaking
juice from ½ key lime

Put Brazil nuts in a medium bowl and cover them with spring water. Soak overnight.
Cook your favorite alkaline pasta.
Prepare your oven and heat it to 350°F/175°C in advance.
Place the cooked pasta in a baking dish and drizzle extra grape seed oil to prevent it sticking to the bottom. Add pasta, flour, nuts, achiote, onion powder, seas salt, grapeseed oil, hempseed milk, water, and lime juice to a blender and blend for 2 to 4 minutes until smooth. Pour the Brazil nut sauce over the macaroni and mix well. Put the dish in the preheated oven and bake for about 30 minutes. Serve and enjoy your macaroni and cheese!

Per Serving: Calories 177; Fat 12g; Sodium 130mg; Carbs 16g; Fiber 3g; Sugar 3g; Protein 3.4g

Vegan Pasta with Cheese and Peas

Prep time: 5 minutes| **Cook time:** 10 minutes| **Serves:** 2

4 ounces maccheroni
¼ cup peas
½ cup vegan mozzarella cheese
½ tablespoon olive oil
1 lemon
Salt and pepper

Set Instant Pot to Sauté. Add the olive oil in the pot and allow it to sizzle. Add maccheroni, peas, lemon, salt and pepper.
Lock the lid and make sure its vent is closed. Set Instant Pot to Manual or Pressure Cook on High Pressure for 10 minutes. When cooking time ends, release pressure and wait for steam to stop before opening lid completely. Add soy mozzarella cheese and stir until everything is combined and coated with sauce.

Per Serving: Calories 176; Fat 8.3g; Sodium 166mg; Carbs 21.8g; Fiber 3.8g; Sugar 3.3g; Protein 5.3g

Mexican Steak Taco

Prep time: 15 minutes| **Cook time:** 15 minutes| **Serves:** 6

2 tablespoons reduced-sodium soy sauce
2 tablespoons freshly squeezed lime juice
2 tablespoons canola oil, divided
3 cloves garlic, minced
2 teaspoons chili powder
1 teaspoon ground cumin
1 teaspoon dried oregano
¾ cup diced red onion
1 ½ pounds skirt steak, cut into ½-inch pieces
12 mini flour tortillas, warmed
½ cup chopped fresh cilantro leaves
1 lime, cut into wedges

Combine lime juice, soy sauce, 1 tablespoon canola oil, garlic, chili powder, cumin, and oregano in a medium bowl.
Combine soy sauce mixture and steak in a gallon-size Ziploc bag or large bowl; marinate for at least one hour up to four hours, rotating the bag regularly.
In a large skillet over medium-high heat, heat the remaining 1 tablespoon canola oil. Cook, often tossing, until steak is browned and the marinade has decreased, about 5-6 minutes, or until the desired doneness is reached.
Serve steak wrapped in tortillas and garnished with onion, cilantro, and lime juice.

Per Serving: Calories 577; Fat 23g; Sodium 1238mg; Carbs 53g; Fiber 3.2g; Sugar 5g; Protein 40g

Basil Pesto Noodles

Prep time: 5 minutes| **Cook time:** 15 minutes| **Serves:** 2

3 tablespoons extra-virgin olive oil
1 bunch fresh basil leaves, rinsed
1 bunch fresh parsley, rinsed
1 bunch fresh cilantro, rinsed
3½ ounces soba buckwheat noodles, cooked according to package directions
Himalayan pink salt
Freshly ground black pepper

In a blender, combine the olive oil, basil, parsley, and cilantro. Blend until smooth.
In a large bowl, combine the cooked noodles and sauce. Toss to coat well, season with salt and pepper, and serve.

Per Serving: Calories 256; Fat 21g; Sodium 436mg; Carbs 16g; Fiber 3g; Sugar 0.7g; Protein 2.8g

Havarti Party Burgers

Prep time: 15 minutes| **Cook time:** 15 minutes| **Serves:** 8

½ pound ground beef
1 envelope ranch salad dressing mix
1 large egg
1 teaspoon water
1 sheet frozen puff pastry, thawed
4 slices Havarti cheese (about 4 ounces), quartered

Preheat oven to 400°F/205°C. In a small bowl, combine beef and dressing mix; toss gently but thoroughly—form eight ½-inch-thick patties.
Cook burgers for 6 to 8 minutes, flip once halfway through cooking or until a thermometer registers 160°F/71°C in a large nonstick pan over medium heat. Take the pan off the heat. Meanwhile, mix egg and water in a small bowl. Unfold puff pastry on a lightly floured board; roll into a 12-inch square. Cut pastry into four 6-inch squares; halve each square to get eight rectangles. Each rectangle should have a burger on one end; top with cheese. Brush egg mixture along the pastry's edges. To wrap the burger, fold the dough over and press edges with a fork to seal.
Transfer to a parchment-lined baking sheet. Tops should be brushed with egg mixture. Bake in your oven until golden brown on the crust, for about 15 to 20 minutes.

Per Serving: Calories 591; Fat 45.2g; Sodium 539mg; Carbs 29.7g; Fiber 1g; Sugar 2g; Protein 16.6g

Zucchini Noodles with Walnuts

Prep time: 30 minutes| **Cook time:** 45 minutes| **Serves:** 3

½ cup walnuts
2 cups basil
2 avocados
4 teaspoons key lime juice
2 large zucchini
2 sliced cherry tomatoes
sea salt to your taste
½ cup water

Use a spiralizer to prepare zucchini noodles.
Then blend the walnuts, basil, avocados, and the key lime juice in a blender until they become smooth.
Combine the cherry tomatoes, the noodles, and the avocado sauce in a mixing bowl.

Per Serving: Calories 313; Fat 28.5g; Sodium 12mg; Carbs 15.5g; Fiber 10g; Sugar 2g; Protein 5.6g

Herbed Kamut Pasta

Prep time: 25 minutes| **Cook time:** 50 minutes| **Serves:** 6

Pasta:
12 ounces kamut spaghetti
1 tablespoon tarragon
1 teaspoon onion powder
1 teaspoon pure sea salt
2 tablespoons grapeseed oil
6 to 8 cups spring water (for boiling the pasta)

Sauce:
2 cups chopped kale
12 chopped cherry tomatoes
½ diced onion
2 cups sliced mushrooms
¼ cup garbanzo bean flour
2 teaspoons onion powder
1 tablespoon oregano
1 teaspoon tarragon
1 teaspoon basil
¼ teaspoon pure sea salt + extra ½ teaspoon
⅛ teaspoon cayenne powder + extra ⅛ teaspoon
2 tablespoons grapeseed oil
2 cups coconut milk
2 cups spring water

Pasta:
In a large pot, bring the spring water to a boil. Add pure sea salt to taste.
Add kamut spaghetti to the boiling water. Then cook the spaghetti for about 8 to 10 minutes until it is al dente.
Drain the pasta and put it in a bowl. Add pure sea salt, tarragon, onion powder and grape seed oil to maximize flavor. Mix seasonings with pasta thoroughly.

Sauce:
Add half the grapeseed oil to a medium pot. Warm on medium heat. Add sliced mushrooms and diced onions to the hot oil. Cook them together for 3 to 5 minutes, stirring occasionally.
Sprinkle ¼ teaspoon of pure sea salt and ⅛ teaspoon of cayenne over the vegetables and stir. Put garbanzo bean flour and another tablespoon of grape seed oil in the pot. Stir until it is well combined with no lumps of dry flour.
Add coconut milk, spring water, ½ teaspoon of pure sea salt, onion powder, oregano, tarragon, and basil and stir. Cook on low heat for 20 minutes until it thickens slightly. Add cooked pasta, chopped tomatoes and kale to the pot. Simmer in the pot for 3 to 5 minutes until kale is cooked then remove from heat.

Per Serving: Calories 389; Fat 29g; Sodium 217mg; Carbs 30g; Fiber 6g; Sugar 6.8g; Protein 7.4g

Awesome Jerk Patties

Prep time: 35 minutes| **Cook time:** 1 hour| **Serves:** 3 to 4

Filling:
1 cup cooked garbanzo beans
½ cup diced green pepper
1 chopped plum tomato
2 cups chopped mushrooms
1 cup chopped butternut squash
½ cup diced onions
1 tablespoon onion powder
1 teaspoon ginger
2 teaspoons thyme
1 tablespoon agave syrup
½ teaspoon cayenne powder
1 teaspoon allspice
¼ teaspoon cloves
1 teaspoon pure sea salt

Crust:
1 ½ cups spelt flour
¼ cup aquafaba
1 teaspoon pure sea salt
⅛ teaspoon ginger powder
1 teaspoon onion powder
1 tablespoon grapeseed oil
1 cup water

Before cooking, heat your oven to 350°F/175°C. Add all vegetables to a food processor, excluding cherry tomatoes. Then pulse a few times to chop them into large pieces. Mix blended vegetables with seasonings and tomatoes in a large bowl. This constitutes the filling for the patties.

In a separate large bowl, combine the spelt flour, grapeseed oil and seasonings. Pour in ½ cup of spring water and knead the dough into a ball, adding more water or flour as needed. Then allow the ball to rest for 5 to 10 minutes.

Knead again for a few minutes then divide it into 8 equal parts. Make them into balls and roll each ball out into a 6- to 7-inch circle. Take a dough circle and place ½ cup of the filling in the center.

Brush all edges of the dough with aquafaba, fold it over in half and seal the edges together with a fork. Repeat the steps until all the dough circles are filled. Lightly coat a baking sheet with a little grapeseed oil. Bake filled patties for about 25 to 30 minutes until golden brown.

Per Serving: Calories 331; Fat 5.5g; Sodium 30mg; Carbs 64.7g; Fiber 10g; Sugar 14.5g; Protein 12.5g

Cabbage Wraps with Strawberries and Nuts

Prep time: 30 minutes| **Cook time:** 0 minutes| **Serves:** 4

½ cup raw pecan nuts, roughly chopped
½ cup fresh sliced strawberries
2 large cabbage leaves
½ ripe avocado, pitted and sliced
1 cup green asparagus spears

Spread out the cabbage sheets on a clean kitchen work surface. Share the asparagus spears among each cabbage leaf and place them on the edge of the leaf.
Share the avocado slices on each leaf and put them on top of the asparagus spears.
Share the strawberries over each leaf and spread on top of the avocado slices.
Share the pecan nuts between each leaf and spread it on the strawberries. Wrap the leaves with all ingredients inside them. Serve with soy sauce

Per Serving: Calories 314; Fat 13.6g; Sodium 156mg; Carbs 48g; Fiber 16g; Sugar 24g; Protein 10.6g

Millet Tabbouleh with Cilantro

Prep time: 15 minutes| **Cook time:** 20 minutes| **Serves:** 6

½ cup lime juice
½ cup cilantro, chopped
5 to 6 drops hot sauce, tabasco
¼ cup and 2 teaspoons olive oil, divided
2 large tomatoes, diced
2 bunches green onions,
2 cucumbers, peeled, and juiced
1 cup millet, rinsed and drained

Add the 2 teaspoons of olive oil in a saucepan and heat over medium heat. Add the millet and fry until it begins to smell fragrant (this takes between three (3) to four (4) minutes). Pour in the saucepan about six (6) cups of water and bring to boil.
Wait for about fifteen (15) minutes. Turn off the heat, wash and rinse under cold water. Drain the millet and transfer to a large bowl. Add cucumbers, tomatoes, lime juice, cilantro, green onions, the ¼ cup oil, and hot sauce. Season with pepper and salt to taste.

Per Serving: Calories 251; Fat 12g; Sodium 8mg; Carbs 32g; Fiber 4g; Sugar 3.7g; Protein 5g

Balsamic Ground Beef

Prep time: 15 minutes| **Cook time:** 10 minutes| **Serves:** 2

1 pound ground beef
¼ cup yellow mustard
1 tablespoon balsamic vinegar
1 tablespoon minced garlic
1 ½ teaspoons soy sauce
1 ½ teaspoons honey
1 ½ teaspoons paprika
⅛ teaspoon ground black pepper

Over medium-high heat, heat a large skillet. In a heated skillet, cook and stir meat until browned and crumbly, 5 to 7 minutes. Reduce heat to a low setting.
In a medium saucepan, mix the ground beef, mustard, balsamic vinegar, garlic, soy sauce, honey, paprika, and pepper; bring to a boil & simmer for approximately 3 minutes, or until cooked through.

Per Serving: Calories 551; Fat 27.2g; Sodium 546mg; Carbs 11g; Fiber 2g; Sugar 6.8g; Protein 62.4g

Mango, Quinoa, and Black Bean Casserole with Sauce

Prep time: 10 minutes| **Cook time:** 25 minutes| **Serves:** 4

2 cups full-fat canned coconut milk
1 cup low-sodium vegetable stock
1 cup quinoa
2 cups black beans, drained and rinsed
1 mango, finely chopped
¼ cup minced fresh mint
A pinch of sea salt, for seasoning

Before cooking, heat the oven to 425°F/220°C. In a casserole dish, combine the stock, milk, and quinoa. Cover and bake for 25 minutes. Remove the dish from the oven. Mix in the beans, mango, and fresh mint. Season with salt and serve.

Per Serving: Calories 639; Fat 32.6g; Sodium 556mg; Carbs 74.8g; Fiber 16g; Sugar 18g; Protein 18.5g

Fried Rice with Mushrooms and Zucchini

Prep time: 15 minutes| **Cook time:** 50 minutes| **Serves:** 2

1 cup cooked wild rice
½ cup sliced mushrooms
½ cup cubed zucchini
½ cup cubed bell peppers
¼ diced onion
pure sea salt, to taste
cayenne powder, to taste
½ tablespoon grapeseed oil

Heat grapeseed oil in a medium pan over medium heat. Add the diced onion to the pan and sauté until golden brown.
Add the zucchini, mushrooms, and bell peppers and cook for 5 more minutes. The vegetables should become a little softer. Add the cooked wild rice and continue sautéing until lightly browned.
Serve and enjoy your healthy fried-rice!

Per Serving: Calories 135; Fat 4g; Sodium 5mg; Carbs 22g; Fiber 3g; Sugar 2.5g; Protein 5g

Ginger-Maple Yam Casserole

Prep time: 10 minutes| **Cook time:** 40 minutes| **Serves:** 4

2 yams, peeled and cut into ½-inch chunks
¼ cup fresh ginger, peeled and grated
2 tablespoons avocado oil
2 tablespoons pure maple syrup
4 teaspoons cardamom
A pinch of sea salt

Before cooking, heat the oven to 375°F/175°C.
In a casserole dish, combine the yams, ginger, oil, maple syrup, cardamom, and salt. Mix well. Cover and bake for 40 minutes.

Per Serving: Calories 155; Fat 7g; Sodium 232mg; Carbs 22g; Fiber 2.6g; Sugar 8.8g; Protein 1g

Gingered Zucchini Noodles

Prep time: 15 minutes| **Cook time:** 25 minutes| **Serves:** 2

½ pound top sirloin steak
4 zucchinis
2 cinnamon sticks
2-star anise
3 whole cloves
4 cups Kettle & Fire beef bone broth
1-inch chunk of fresh ginger, sliced
1 tablespoon soy sauce (use tamari sauce or coconut aminos for a gluten-free version)
1 tablespoon fish sauce

For the Toppings:
2 handfuls of bean sprouts
herb mix (cilantro, basil, or both)
1 jalapeño pepper, sliced (optional)
2 stems green onion, chopped
hoisin sauce, sriracha, and lime wedges for serving

Freeze the sirloin steak for 15 minutes to facilitate slicing.
To make zucchini noodles, use a spiralizer or a julienne peeler. Distribute the zoodles evenly between two large serving dishes.
Toast the cinnamon sticks, star anise, and cloves in a medium skillet over medium heat until aromatic. In a saucepan, combine bone broth, ginger, soy sauce, and fish sauce. Raise the heat to low and simmer. Allow 10 minutes for the spices to properly infuse the stock.
Remove the steak out of the freezer and slice it thinly. Divide the meat into two parts and put the serving dishes on top of the zoodles.
Once the soup is finished, split it in half and ladle it into the serving dishes. Instantly, the steak will begin to cook, and the color will change.
Serve the pho topped with bean sprouts, fresh herbs, sliced pepper, and green onion, drizzled with Sriracha or/and hoisin sauce, and squeezed with lime juice.

Per Serving: Calories 647; Fat 25.8g; Sodium 2686mg; Carbs 42g; Fiber 13g; Sugar 13.8g; Protein 65.6g

Garlic Chicken and Asparagus Fry

Prep time: 15 minutes| **Cook time:** 15 minutes| **Serves:** 4

1 ½ pounds skinless chicken breast cubes
kosher salt, to taste
½ cup chicken broth with reduced sodium
2 tablespoons Shoyu or soy sauce with low sodium coconut amino acids for gluten-free
2 teaspoons cornstarch, arrowroot powder, or tapioca starch
2 tablespoons water
1 tablespoon grapeseed or canola oil, split
1 bunch asparagus, clipped ends, sliced into 2-inch sections
6 garlic cloves, chopped
1 tablespoon freshly grated ginger
3 tablespoons freshly squeezed lemon juice
pepper, nitrogen-fresh, to taste

Season the chicken lightly with salt.
Chicken broth and soy sauce should be mixed together in a small bowl before being served.
In a second small bowl, whisk together the cornstarch and water.
Cook 1 teaspoon of the oil in a large nonstick wok over medium-high heat until heated, then add the asparagus and cook until tender-crisp, about 3 to 4 minutes.
Cook until the garlic and ginger are browned, about 1 minute. Place aside.
Increase to high heat and add 1 teaspoon oil and half of the chicken; cook until browned and cooked through, about 4 minutes per side.
Removing and setting aside, repeat with the remainder of the oil and chicken. Place aside.
Simmer for about 1-½ minutes after bringing to a boil.
Lemon juice and cornstarch mixture should be added at this point until smooth; add the chicken and asparagus back to the wok and toss well; remove from heat and serve.

Per Serving: Calories 266; Fat 8g; Sodium 343mg; Carbs 6g; Fiber 0.7g; Sugar 1g; Protein 40g

Stuffed Potato Cake

Prep time: 15 minutes| **Cook time:** 30 minutes| **Serves:** 4

For the Cakes:
Salt
1 bay leaf
10 medium gold potatoes
1 cup potato starch plus more for dusting

For the Stuffing:
Coconut oil for panfrying
Salt and freshly ground black pepper
1 medium onion, chopped
2 tablespoons olive oil
¾ cup dried green lentils (preferably French lentils)- cooked

Combine the 7 cups of water, potatoes and bay leaf in a large pot and boil until the potatoes are tender. Poke with a fork to ensure they are cooked. Rinse the potatoes under cold water when done; the skins will peel off easily. Now mash the potatoes until smooth and then add the potato starch, stir to make dough. Add more potato starch if the dough feels too sticky.
For the stuffing, add olive oil to a sauté pan and place over medium high heat.
Add in onions and cook as you stir for 5 minutes. Add in the lentils together with pepper and salt (to taste) and cook for 2 minutes. Set aside.
To make the cakes, scoop about 3 tablespoons of the dough on your hand and press it into your palm.
Add a spoonful of stuffing on top of the dough and fold it over to close it. Shape it into a round disk. Now add coconut oil to a skillet and heat over medium heat. Cook the potato cakes on both sides until golden, roughly 4 minutes per side.

Per Serving: Calories 669; Fat 11g; Sodium 38mg; Carbs 125.7g; Fiber 17g; Sugar 6g; Protein 21g

Chapter 5 Dinner Recipes

Quinoa-Fruit Bowl

Prep time: 25 minutes | **Cook time:** 15 minutes | **Serves:** 2-4

1 cup quinoa
1 cup salsa, any store brand
1 cup water
1 (15 ounce) can black beans, thoroughly drained and rinsed
2 cups corn kernels, thawed if using frozen
Sea salt and pepper
1 lime, zested and juiced
½ cup cilantro, chopped
1 romaine lettuce heart, chopped
8-ounce grape tomatoes, sliced lengthwise
½ cup red onion, diced
1 avocado, sliced

Add quinoa, salsa, water, beans, corn, sea salt, and pepper to instant pot.
Close lid and seal. Let them cook in Rice mode on low pressure for 12 minutes.
After cooking, allow pressure to release on its own; then fluff quinoa with a fork.
Add lime zest and juice, cilantro, and more salt and pepper if needed to the quinoa. Toss well.
Serve them on the plate, top with lettuce, tomatoes, red onion, and avocado. Enjoy!

Per Serving: Calories 354; Fat 11.7g; Sodium 666mg; Carbs 57.08g; Fiber 12g; Sugar 8.56g; Protein 11.65g

Keto Avocado and Tahini Bowl

Prep time: 10 minutes | **Cook time:** 0 | **Serves:** 4

1 large avocado, destoned and diced
2 tablespoons of lime juice
2 tablespoons of olive oil
2 cans of tuna, flaked
2 tablespoons of fresh cilantro, finely chopped
2 tablespoons of tahini sauce
3 tablespoons of gluten-free tamari sauce
1 tablespoon of sesame oil

Thoroughly mix the tahini sauce, gluten-free tamari sauce, and sesame oil in a bowl.
Whisk the lime juice, cilantro, olive oil, and tuna in another bowl.
Add the avocado to a serving bowl, top with tuna and paste. Enjoy.

Per Serving: Calories 250; Fat 18.35g; Sodium 366mg; Carbs 6.45g; Fiber 3.8g; Sugar 1.35g; Protein 17.43g

Stuffed Portobello Mushrooms

Prep time: 15 minutes | **Cook time:** 50 minutes | **Serves:** 4

For Mushroom:
8 large (4-inch wide) trimmed Portobello mushroom stems
kosher salt and freshly crushed black pepper
extra virgin olive oil

For Sautéed Spinach:
1 tablespoon olive oil extra virgin
6 ounces' baby spinach
1 shallot
kosher salt, and freshly ground black pepper

For Crunchy Breadcrumb Topping:
2 tablespoons salted butter
1 finely diced shallot
½ cup panko breadcrumbs
1 finely minced garlic clove
kosher salt and freshly ground black pepper

For Assembly:
1½ cups for assembly (12 ounces) marinara sauce (store-bought or handmade)
4 ounces' goat cheese, straight from the refrigerator

To make the mushroom:
Preheat the oven to 450°F/230°C.
Lightly spray a regular sheet pan with olive oil.
Evenly arrange the mushrooms on the sheet pan, stem side up; lightly brush them with olive oil, and season them with salt and black pepper.
Roast the mushrooms in the preheated oven for 15 to 25 minutes or until soft (If any moisture accumulates in the mushroom caps, gently drain and discard).
Transfer the mushrooms to a large platter, and set aside for later use.

To make the spinach:
Heat the oil in a sauté pan over medium-low heat; sauté the sliced shallots for 3 to 4 minutes until tender and transparent.
Increase the heat to medium-high heat, add the young spinach and sauté until the spinach is barely wilted.
Transfer the spinach to another platter, and season with salt and black pepper.

To make the crispy breadcrumb toasted:
Melt the butter in a small sauté pan over medium heat.
When the butter starts to crackle, turn off the heat, and add the chopped shallots, salt, and stir for 1 to 2 minutes.
Add the panko breadcrumbs and minced garlic, and toast for 3 to 4 minutes, stirring regularly, or until the breadcrumbs are light golden; transfer the breadcrumbs to a shallow bowl, and season with salt and pepper.
Line the same sheet pan with parchment paper, and arrange the roasted mushrooms, stem side up evenly around the sheet pan's center so that they are just touching.
Fill each mushroom halfway with marinara sauce, and apportion the sautéed spinach between the mushrooms, spooning it over the sauce.
Make the goat cheese into 12-inch thick chunks (roughly half an ounce), but try to retain them a roughly round shape.
Gently press the goat cheese slices in the panko breadcrumb topping on both sides, and place one on each mushroom. Sprinkle the remaining breadcrumb mixture over the mushrooms.
Bake them at 425°F/220°C for 10 to 15 minutes until the breadcrumbs are golden brown and the goat cheese is just beginning to soften.
Serve warm.

Per Serving: Calories 247; Fat 16.54g; Sodium 1014mg; Carbs 14.11g; Fiber 3.5g; Sugar 6.57g; Protein 13.57g

Popcorn Shrimp in Milk

Prep time: 20 minutes | **Cook time:** 15 minutes | **Serves:** 4

1-pound small shrimp peeled and deveined
1¼ cups of all-purpose flour
2 teaspoons salt plus more for serving
½ teaspoon paprika smoked or regular
¼ teaspoon pepper
¼ teaspoon garlic powder
1 egg
¼ cup of milk
Vegetable oil for frying
2 teaspoons chopped fresh parsley

Combine the flour, salt, paprika, pepper, and garlic powder in a medium bowl.
Beat the egg with milk in a small bowl.
Pat the shrimp dry, put them in a big bowl, and coat them with ¼ cup of the flour mixture. Dip each shrimp into the milk mixture, and then dust them with the remaining flour mixture.
In a large deep pot, heat 3-4 inches of vegetable oil to 375°F/190°C. Cook 8 to 10 shrimp chunks at a time for 2 to 3 minutes until golden brown, stirring occasionally.
When cooked, take the shrimp out, and put them on a paper towel.
Do the same with the remaining shrimp.
Serve the shrimp on a serving plate, garnish with parsley and enjoy.

Per Serving: Calories 326; Fat 11.62g; Sodium 743mg; Carbs 32.27g; Fiber 1.2g; Sugar 1.1g; Protein 21.48g

Lemon Rosemary Salmon

Prep time: 20 minutes | **Cook time:** 10 minutes | **Serves:** 4

1 lemon, thinly sliced
4 sprigs of fresh rosemary
2 salmon fillets, bones, and skin removed
coarse salt as need
1 tablespoon olive oil, or as needed

Preheat the oven to 400°F/200°C.
Season the salmon fillets with 2 rosemary sprigs and lemon wedges.
Arrange half of the lemon slices in a single layer on the baking pan, top them with 2 rosemary sprigs and salmon fillets, and then drizzle with extra-virgin olive oil.
Bake the salmon fillets for 20 minutes until they are readily flake.
Serve and enjoy.

Per Serving: Calories 272; Fat 10.97g; Sodium 177mg; Carbs 1.18g; Fiber 0.3g; Sugar 0.3g; Protein 39.98g

Honey Zucchini and Leeks

Prep time: 15 minutes | **Cook time:** 20 minutes | **Serves:** 4

2 leeks, finely chopped
2 zucchinis, finely chopped
⅓ cup water
2 tablespoons olive oil
1 tablespoon honey
½ teaspoon dried basil
Pinch of salt
⅛ teaspoon ground black pepper

Add all the ingredients to the skillet, and then bring to a boil.
After boiling, reduce heat and simmer them for 15 minutes until liquid evaporates.
Then, stir mixture for 2 to 3 minutes until leeks and carrots are lightly browned.
Serve and enjoy.

Per Serving: Calories 105; Fat 6.91g; Sodium 49mg; Carbs 10.98g; Fiber 0.9g; Sugar 6.12g; Protein 0.88g

Tofu Strips with Vegetables

Prep time: 5 minutes | **Cook time:** 10 minutes | **Serves:** 4

2 tablespoons olive oil
1½-pound tofu, cut into strips
Salt and ground black pepper to taste
2 tablespoon Tex-Mex seasoning
1 small iceberg lettuce, chopped
2 large tomatoes, deseeded and chopped
2 avocados, halved, pitted, and chopped
1 green bell pepper, deseeded and thinly sliced
1 yellow onion, thinly sliced
4 tablespoon fresh cilantro leaves
½ cup shredded dairy- free parmesan cheese blend
1 cup plain unsweetened yogurt

Season the tofu strips with Tex-Mex seasoning, salt, and black pepper.
Heat the olive oil in a medium skillet over medium heat.
Add the seasoned tofu strips to the oil, and fry them on both sides until golden and cooked, for 5 to 10 minutes. Transfer to a plate.
Divide the lettuce among 4 serving bowls, share the tofu on top, and then add the tomatoes, avocados, bell pepper, onion, cilantro, and cheese.
Top them with dollops of plain yogurt, and serve immediately with low carb tortillas.

Per Serving: Calories 486; Fat 32.48g; Sodium 1343mg; Carbs 31.78g; Fiber 10.7g; Sugar 10.44g; Protein 24.38g

Fish Tacos

Prep time: 15 minutes | **Cook time:** 6 minutes | **Serves:** 4

For the fish:
1-pound cod, tilapia, halibut, or other white fish fillets
2 to 3 teaspoons chili powder, enough to coat the fish
1 teaspoon salt

For the fish taco sauce:
½ cup of sour cream
¼ cup of mayonnaise
3 to 4 tablespoons lime juice (from 2 limes)
1 teaspoon warm sauce, optional

To assemble:
½ little head red cabbage, shredded (about 4 cups of)
12 taco-sized corn or flour tortillas
1 avocado, sliced
4 radishes, thinly sliced
4 spring onions, thinly sliced
⅓ cup of roughly chopped cilantro

Make the fish taco sauce:
Combine the sour cream, mayonnaise, lime juice, and spicy sauce (optional) in a small bowl.

Make the red cabbage slaw:
Mix the shredded cabbage and 3 tablespoons taco sauce in a medium bowl to coat the cabbage well.

Warm the tortillas:
Heat the tortillas one at a time for approximately 30 seconds on each side in a dry pan over medium-high heat.
Alternatively, wrap 1–3 tortillas in a moist paper towel and microwave for 30 seconds until heated through.
Transfer the tortillas to a plate, and cover with a clean dish towel to keep hot.

Season the fish:
Sprinkle the fish with chili powder and salt on both sides.

Cook the fish:
Preheat a big cast iron or nonstick pan over medium-high heat.
When the pan is heated, add 1 tablespoon olive oil and tilt the pan to coat the bottom thoroughly.
Cook the fish for 4 minutes on each side. The fish is done when it is opaque throughout and readily breaks apart.
Serve the tacos:
Transfer the fried fillets to a dish, and carefully break the fish into big bits using a fork.
Assemble the tacos by layering a few fish, cabbage slaw, desired toppings, and a dab of taco sauce on top. Enjoy.

Per Serving: Calories 307; Fat 16.28g; Sodium 1140mg; Carbs 20.54g; Fiber 6.5g; Sugar 4.01g; Protein 22.3g

Chicken-Broccoli Stuffed Peppers

Prep time: 25 minutes | **Cook time:** 40 minutes | **Serves:** 4

5 bell peppers
10 ounces cooked chicken breast
1 bunch broccoli
1 cup grated gouda cheese
¼ cup whipped cream
1-2 tablespoon chopped fresh parsley (optional)
½ teaspoon red pepper flakes
½ teaspoon garlic powder
14 teaspoons paprika
¼ teaspoon more salt to taste
1 minced garlic clove
½ teaspoon butter
¼ to ½ cup cheddar cheese for garnish

Preheat oven to 350°F/175°C.
Slice off bell peppers' tops, and then cut in half lengthwise.
Remove the stem from the broccoli until you have three broccoli crowns, save the stem for later use.
Prepare a huge dish of ice and water.
Bring a pot of water to boil, and add the bell peppers to the boiled water; blanch the bell peppers for 3 minutes in boiling water, then immediately plunge into ice water and prevent mushy peppers.
Pat them dry and set aside for later use.
Simply submerge broccoli in the same boiling water, and blanch for 4 minutes until brilliant green and tender.
Strain broccoli, dip them in ice water, pat them dry, and set aside for later use.
Place the cooked chicken breast and broccoli on a cutting board, and coarsely chop them.
Mix the chicken, broccoli, gouda cheese, cream, garlic powder, paprika, and salt in a large bowl.
Heat butter and minced garlic clove for 30 seconds to soften; add the buttered garlic to the chicken mixture, and mix well.
Fill each pepper half with the mixture; arrange the peppers on a rimmed baking pan lined with parchment paper, and cover the pan with foil.
Bake the peppers in the preheated oven for 15 to 25 minutes.
Remove the foil and resume baking them for 1 to 2 minutes until the cheese is brown and bubbling.
Serve the pepper on the plates, garnish with parsley and red pepper flakes. Enjoy.

Per Serving: Calories 409; Fat 20.44g; Sodium 520mg; Carbs 21.8g; Fiber 7.8g; Sugar 7.34g; Protein 39.28g

Veggie Beef Bacon Burgers

Prep time: 25 minutes | **Cook time:** 10 minutes | **Serves:** 8

2 large carrots, grated
1 large onion, grated
1 cup of mashed potato flakes
2 eggs, lightly beaten
1 garlic clove, minced
1 teaspoon salt
Pepper as need
2 pounds ground beef
8 bacon strips
8 lettuce leaves, optional
8 hamburger buns, split, optional

Combine the carrots, onion, potato flakes, eggs, garlic, salt, and pepper in a mixing bowl.
Mix beef with the mixture gradually, then make them into 8 patties.
Wrap each patty with one bacon strip, and secure with toothpicks.
Cook the patties in a large pan until the meat is no longer pink, and each bacon is crunchy.
Discard the toothpicks, serve the patties on hamburger buns (optional).

Per Serving: Calories 425; Fat 16.97g; Sodium 674mg; Carbs 29.04g; Fiber 2.4g; Sugar 4.88g; Protein 37.24g

Quinoa Vegetable Bowl

Prep time: 10 minutes | **Cook time:** 35 minutes | **Serves:** 4

1 (28-ounce) can crushed tomatoes
1 cup low-sodium vegetable stock
1 cup quinoa
1 tablespoon dried basil
A pinch of sea salt, plus more for seasoning
1 cup halved snap peas
½ cup coarsely chopped yellow bell peppers
½ cup thinly sliced white mushrooms
Freshly ground black pepper, for seasoning

Mix the vegetable stock, tomatoes, quinoa, basil, and salt in a stockpot.
Cover the pot, and bring to a boil over high heat.
After boiling, reduce the heat to low, and simmer the food for 20 minutes.
Add the peas, peppers, and mushrooms to the pot, and stir well.
Cover the pot and let simmer for 5 to 10 minutes more.
Season the food with salt and black pepper before serving.

Per Serving: Calories 207; Fat 3.36g; Sodium 305mg; Carbs 37.96g; Fiber 7.4g; Sugar 7.41g; Protein 8.73g

Baby Courgettes in Vegetable Stock

Prep time: 13 minutes | **Cook time:** 17 minutes | **Serves:** 3

2 cups baby courgettes
3 tablespoons vegetable stock
2 tablespoons apple cider vinegar
1 tablespoon light brown sugar
4 spring onions, finely sliced
1-piece fresh gingerroot, grated
1 teaspoon corn flour
2 teaspoons water
One orange
½ lemon
Salt

Pour the water into the stockpot, add salt as needed and bring to a boil.
Add courgettes to the pot, and boil them for 5 minutes.
Add vegetable stock, apple cider vinegar, brown sugar, sprig onions, gingerroot, lemon juice and rind, and orange juice and rind to another pan, and bring to a boil.
After boiling, lower the heat and simmer them for 3 minutes.
Mix the corn flour with water in a bowl. Pour into the onion sauce, and then resume stirring until the sauce thickens.
Drain courgettes and transfer to the serving dish. Spoon over the sauce. Toss to coat courgettes. Enjoy.

Per Serving: Calories 167; Fat 13.89g; Sodium 58mg; Carbs 11.14g; Fiber 1.5g; Sugar 7.54g; Protein 1.58g

Cucumber Shrimp

Prep time: 5 minutes | **Cook time:** 10 minutes | **Serves:** 4

one large cucumber, peeled and sliced into ½-inch round slices
10–15 large shrimp (defrosted if frozen)
1 teaspoon fresh ginger, grated
salt and pepper as need
1 tablespoon coconut oil

Heat coconut oil in a frying pan over medium heat.
Sauté the ginger and cucumber for 2-3 minutes.
Add the shrimp to the pan, and cook them for 7 minutes or until they become pink and are no longer transparent.
Season with salt. Serve and enjoy.

Per Serving: Calories 47; Fat 3.6g; Sodium 100mg; Carbs 1.33g; Fiber 0.2g; Sugar 0.59g; Protein 2.62g

Seitan with Avocado Puree

Prep time: 5 minutes | **Cook time:** 10 minutes | **Serves:** 4

1 white onion, finely chopped
¼ cup vegetable stock
3 tablespoons coconut oil
3 tablespoons tamari sauce
3 tablespoons chili pepper
1 tablespoon red wine vinegar
Salt and ground black pepper to taste
2-pound Seitan
1 large avocado, halved and pitted
½ lemon, juiced

Add the onion, vegetable stock, coconut oil, tamari sauce, chili pepper, red wine vinegar, salt, black pepper, and seitan to a large pot, cover the pot, and cook the food over low heat for 2 hours.
Scoop the avocado pulp into a bowl, add the lemon juice; mash the avocado into a puree.
Turn the heat off, and mix the onion mixture with the avocado puree, then season them with salt and black pepper.
Spoon onto a serving platter and serve warm.

Per Serving: Calories 379; Fat 28.61g; Sodium 128mg; Carbs 17.31g; Fiber 5.5g; Sugar 4.92g; Protein 20.91g

Salmon Onion Stew

Prep time: 10 minutes | **Cook time:** 15 minutes | **Serves:** 8

1 or 2 can regular pink salmon, deboned, and skin removed but save the broth
1 med onion chopped small
1 or 2 stick butter
32 or 64 ounces' regular milk
salt and pepper as need

Quarter the onion, and cut it finely but not mushily in a small chopper.
Melt the butter in a stew pot over medium-low bowl.
Sauté the chopped onion over medium heat until translucent and tender; add the salmon, combine thoroughly.
Slowly pour in the milk, and add the fish bone, and skin; decrease the heat to slow to avoid scalding it.
Stir every few minutes, bring to a boil.
Season the food with pepper and salt. Serve warm.

Per Serving: Calories 570; Fat 14.32g; Sodium 1049mg; Carbs 59.77g; Fiber 0.1g; Sugar 59.32g; Protein 50.32g

Grilled Tempeh and Pineapple with Vegetables

Prep time: 12 minutes | **Cook time:** 16 minutes | **Serves:** 3

10-ounce tempeh, sliced
1 red bell pepper, quartered
¼ pineapple, sliced into rings
6-ounce green beans
1 tablespoon coconut aminos
2½ tablespoons orange juice, freshly squeeze
1 ½ tablespoon lemon juice, freshly squeezed
1 tablespoon extra-virgin olive oil
¼ cup hoisin sauce

Whisk olive oil, orange and lemon juices, coconut aminos, and hoisin sauce in a bowl; marinate the sliced tempeh with the mixture.
Heat the grill pan over medium high flame.
Once hot, transfer the marinated tempeh to the grill pan, and grill them for 2 to 3 minutes until browned all over. Grill the sliced pineapples alongside the tempeh, then transfer them directly onto the serving platter. Place the grilled tempeh beside the grilled pineapple, and cover with aluminum foil to keep warm.
Add the green beans and bell peppers to the marinade bowl, and coat with the marinade.
Add them to the grill pan, and grill them until fork tender and slightly charred.
Transfer the grilled vegetables to the serving platter, and arrange artfully with the tempeh and pineapple. Enjoy.

Per Serving: Calories 264; Fat 13.04g; Sodium 400mg; Carbs 22.18g; Fiber 1g; Sugar 8.35g; Protein 18.69g

Sautéed Chicken Breast

Prep time: 25 minutes | **Cook time:** 20 minutes | **Serves:** 2

1 chicken breast (½-pound), minced or chopped very small
2 cloves of garlic, minced or finely diced
1 chili pepper, diced (optional)
1 cup of (1 large bunch) basil leaves, finely chopped
2 tablespoons water
1 tablespoon gluten-free tamari sauce (use coconut aminos for AIP)
1 tablespoon coconut oil
Salt as need

Add 1 tablespoon coconut oil, minced garlic to a large saucepan, and cook.
When the garlic begins to yellow, add the chili (optional), and stir in the chicken mince.
Keep cooking, add water as needed until the chicken is cooked through.
Add the tamari sauce, salt, and basil leaves to the saucepan, and cook.
You can serve this dish with rice.

Per Serving: Calories 324; Fat 20.29g; Sodium 235mg; Carbs 3.73g; Fiber 0.6g; Sugar 1.53g; Protein 31.02g

Spring-Thyme Chicken Stew

Prep time: 25 minutes | **Cook time:** 10 minutes | **Serves:** 4

1-pound small red potatoes, halved
1 large onion, finely chopped
¾ cup of shredded carrots
6 garlic cloves, minced
2 teaspoons grated lemon zest
2 teaspoons dried thyme
½ teaspoon salt
¼ teaspoon black pepper
1½-pound boneless skinless chicken thighs, cut into 1-inch pieces
2 cups of reduced-sodium chicken broth, divided
2 bay leaves
3 tablespoons all-purpose flour
2 tablespoons minced fresh parsley

Combine the potatoes, onion, and carrots: garlic, lemon zest, thyme, salt, and pepper in the pressure cooker, and then arrange chicken on top.
Mix 1¾ cups broth and bay leave in a medium bowl, and then pour in the pressure cooker.
Cook them in the pressure cooker on High pressure for 5 minutes.
When done, allow the pressure to release rapidly (the chicken should reach an internal temperature of 170°F). 5. Discard the bay leaves, transfer the chicken to the plate and keep warm.
Mix the flour and the remaining broth in a small bowl, then stir in the pressure cooker. Simmer the mixture for 1 to 2 minutes on Sauté mode. Then, reintroduce the chicken-vegetable mixture to pressure cooker, reheat until heated through.
Garnish this dish with parsley, and enjoy.

Per Serving: Calories 528; Fat 13.14g; Sodium 900mg; Carbs 31.11g; Fiber 3.6g; Sugar 4.17g; Protein 67.97g

Chorizo and Brown Rice Bowls

Prep time: 30 minutes | **Cook time:** 50 minutes | **Serves:** 4

2 tablespoons olive oil
2 cups chopped soy chorizo
1 teaspoon taco seasoning
2 green bell peppers, deseeded and sliced
1 cup brown rice
2 cups vegetable broth
Salt to taste
¼ cup salsa
1 lemon, zested and juiced
1 (8-ounce) can pinto beans, drained and rinsed
1 (7-ounce) can sweet corn kernels, drained
2 green onions, chopped
2 tablespoons freshly chopped parsley

Heat the olive oil in a medium pot, and cook the soy chorizo for 5 minutes until golden brown.
Add the taco seasoning and bell peppers to the pot, and cook for 3 minutes until the peppers slightly soften.
Stir in the brown rice, vegetable broth, salt, salsa, and lemon zest. Cover the pot and cook the food for 15 until the rice is tender and all the liquid is absorbed.
Mix in the lemon juice, pinto beans, corn kernels, and green onions, and then allow them warm for 3 to 5 minutes.
Serve the food on a plate, garnish with the parsley and enjoy.

Per Serving: Calories 336; Fat 14.38g; Sodium 691mg; Carbs 42.62g; Fiber 7.6g; Sugar 8.55g; Protein 12.55g

Salmon and Caramelized Veggies

Prep time: 25 minutes | **Cook time:** 40 minutes | **Serves:** 4

10 Brussels sprouts, trimmed and halved
6 slender rainbow carrots, trimmed and peeled
12-ounce a variety of tiny colored potatoes
½ standard eggplant, roughly 2-inch slices
2-3 jalapeno peppers, divided lengthwise
2-3 tablespoons olive oil
Salt
Freshly crushed black pepper
4 salmon slices (about ⅓ pound each)
9 thin lemon slices
Honey or marmalade
Thyme or dill, fresh

Preheat the oven to 425°F/220°C.
Mix the Brussels sprouts, carrots, potatoes, eggplant, and jalapeno peppers with salt, black pepper, and olive oil in a bowl.
Arranged the vegetables in a single layer on the baking sheet, then cook them in the preheated oven for 10 to 15 minutes.
Lightly season the salmon slices with salt and honey (optional), and top them with lemon slices.
Take out the baking sheet, allow space for the salmon slices, and tuck them amid the vegetables.
Cook them in the oven for 20 minutes until the salmon slices are opaque and the vegetables are caramelized and soft.
Sprinkle them with fresh thyme or dill before serving.

Per Serving: Calories 426; Fat 14.88g; Sodium 196mg; Carbs 41.8g; Fiber 9g; Sugar 13.01g; Protein 35.07g

Breaded Cod Fillets

Prep time: 10 minutes | **Cook time:** 20 minutes | **Serves:** 4

4 cod filets (⅓-pound every)
¼ cup of cashew flour
¼ cup of coconut flour
2 tablespoons coconut flakes
3 tablespoons garlic powder
1 tablespoon onion powder
1 egg, whisked
Salt
2 tablespoons ghee
3 cloves garlic, minced
Coconut oil for greasing baking tray

Preheat oven to 425°F/220°C.
Beat the egg in a mixing dish.
Mix the cashew flour, coconut flour, coconut flakes, garlic powder, onion powder, and salt in another bowl.
Wrap aluminum foil around a baking pan and grease with coconut oil.
Dip the cod fillet in the whisked egg, then in the flour mixture.
Arrange the coated cod fillets in a single layer on the baking pan, and bake them for 15 to 20 minutes until they are readily flake.
Light melt the ghee and cook the minced garlic in a saucepan over medium-low heat.
Top the fillets with the garlic-ghee sauce, and enjoy.

Per Serving: Calories 314; Fat 16.75g; Sodium 578mg; Carbs 14.26g; Fiber 1.9g; Sugar 3.18g; Protein 27.61g

Curry Chicken Breast with Potatoes

Prep time: 30 minutes | **Cook time:** 5-6 hours | **Serves:** 4

2 medium potatoes, peeled and cubed
1 small onion, chopped
1-pound boneless skinless chicken breast halves
2 teaspoons canola oil
1 cup of light coconut milk
4 teaspoons curry powder
1 garlic clove, minced
1 teaspoon reduced-sodium chicken bouillon granules
¼ teaspoon salt
¼ teaspoon black pepper
2 cups of hot cooked rice
Optional: cilantro, shredded coconut, chopped peanuts, and thinly sliced red chilies

Heat canola oil in a large nonstick pan over medium heat; add chicken, and cook for 3-5 minutes until lightly browned.
Transfer the chicken to a slow cooker, and add the potatoes and onion to the slow cooker.
Mix coconut milk, curry powder, garlic, chicken bouillon granules, salt, and black pepper in a small bowl, and then pour the mixture over the chicken and vegetables.
Cook them in the slow cooker on low for 5 to 6 hours.
When done, slice the chicken. Enjoy this dish with rice, optionally garnish this dish with cilantro, coconut, peanuts, and chilies.

Per Serving: Calories 575; Fat 20.27g; Sodium 225mg; Carbs 65.81g; Fiber 6.8g; Sugar 4.34g; Protein 33.46g

Veggie Skewers with Corn

Prep time: 20 minutes | **Cook time:** 15 minutes | **Serves:** 4-6

1 red onion, peeled, chopped
2 tablespoons avocado oil
2 Portobello mushrooms, chopped
1 sweet potato, chopped
2 bell peppers, chopped
6 baby red potatoes, quartered
Salt and black pepper, to taste
4 ears corn

Preheat the oven to 375°F/190°C.
Add the sweet potato, quartered baby red potatoes, and water to a cooking pot. Bring to a boil, and then cook the potatoes for 10 minutes until lightly tender.
When done, drain the water and let cool a bit.
Thread the vegetables onto skewers, brush them evenly with oil, and then season the vegetables generously with salt and pepper on each side.
Cook the vegetables in the preheated oven for about 10-15 minutes until tender and cooked through. Flip the skewers and add the corn to them halfway through.
When done, serve and enjoy with the desired sauce.

Per Serving: Calories 222; Fat 5.68g; Sodium 69mg; Carbs 40.72g; Fiber 4.9g; Sugar 7.43g; Protein 5.75g

Chapter 6 Snack and Appetizer Recipes

Tomato Muffin Pizzas

Prep time: 10 minutes | **Cook time:** 15 minutes | **Serves:** 4

¼ cup refried beans, vegan
2 tablespoons tomato, diced
2 English muffins, split in half
¼ cup onion, sliced
⅓ cup vegan cheese, shredded
1 small jalapeno, sliced
⅓ cup roasted tomato salsa
½ avocado, diced and tossed in lemon juice

Add the refried beans to the muffin bread. Sprinkle with shredded vegan cheese followed by the veggie toppings.
Transfer the food to a baking sheet; bake in oven at 400°F/205°C for 12 minutes until the top becomes bubbly.
Take out from the oven and let them cool at room temperature.
Top with avocado. Enjoy!

Per Serving: Calories 161; Fat 6.97g; Sodium 194mg; Carbs 21.19g; Fiber 4.7g; Sugar 4.46g; Protein 6.06g

Shortbread Vanilla Cookies

Prep time: 10 minutes | **Cook time:** 20 minutes | **Serves:** 6

2½ cups almond flour
6 tablespoons nut butter
½ cup erythritol
1 teaspoon vanilla essence

Line the cookie sheet with parchment paper.
Preheat your oven to 350°F.
Beat butter and erythritol in a bowl until fluffy; stir in vanilla essence and almond flour, mix them until crumbly. Spoon out 1 tablespoon of cookie dough onto the cookie sheet, add more dough to make as many cookies.
Bake the cookies for 15 minutes until brown.
Serve warm.

Per Serving: Calories 176; Fat 11.77g; Sodium 92mg; Carbs 18.13g; Fiber 0.1g; Sugar 18g; Protein 0.23g

Sautéed Banana Hash Browns

Prep time: 15 minutes | **Cook time:** 6 minutes | **Serves:** 6

3 green bananas, peeled and chopped
¼ cup onion
¼ cup green pepper
1 plum tomato, diced
1 teaspoon sea salt
1 teaspoon oregano
½ teaspoon cayenne powder
Grapeseed oil for frying

Mix all the ingredients except the grapeseed oil in a bowl.
Press the Sauté button on the Instant Pot and heat the oil.
Heat 1 tablespoon of the mixture in the Instant Pot for 3 minutes on all sides, flatten to form a small pancake.
Do the same to the remaining mixture.
Serve warm.

Per Serving: Calories 81; Fat 2.53g; Sodium 389mg; Carbs 15.56g; Fiber 1.9g; Sugar 8.63g; Protein 0.84g

Homemade Zucchini Strips

Prep time: 10 minutes | **Cook time:** 6 minutes | **Serves:** 4

3 zucchinis, sliced thinly lengthwise or into large strips
¼ cup date sugar
¼ cup spring water
1 tablespoon sea salt
1 tablespoon onion powder
½ teaspoon cayenne pepper powder
½ teaspoon ground ginger
1 tablespoon liquid smoke
Grapeseed oil for frying

Mix all the ingredients except the grapeseed oil in a bowl.
Allow the zucchini strips to marinate for at least 2 hours in the fridge.
Heat the grapeseed oil in the instant pot on Sauté mode.
Fry the marinated zucchini strips for 3 minutes on each side until crispy.
Serve warm.

Per Serving: Calories 79; Fat 1.69g; Sodium 617mg; Carbs 15.37g; Fiber 2g; Sugar 12.78g; Protein 2.3g

Fried Sausage Links

Prep time: 15 minutes | **Cook time:** 6 minutes | **Serves:** 6

2 cups garbanzos beans flour
1 cup chopped mushrooms
½ cup chopped onions
1 tomato, chopped
1 teaspoon oregano
1 teaspoon sea salt
1 teaspoon ground sage
1 teaspoon dill, chopped
½ teaspoon cayenne pepper powder
Grapeseed oil for frying

Mix all the ingredients except the grapeseed oil in the bowl.
Form the mixture into small logs of sausages, and then place them inside the fridge to set for at least 30 minutes.
Heat the grapeseed oil, then carefully add the sausage links to the hot oil, and cook for 3 minutes on all sides.

Per Serving: Calories 185; Fat 2.81g; Sodium 391mg; Carbs 34.55g; Fiber 1.9g; Sugar 1.57g; Protein 5.19g

Wheat Coconut Crackers

Prep time: 10 minutes | **Cook time:** 20 minutes | **Serves:** 4

1¾ cups wheat flour
1½ cups coconut flour
¾ teaspoon sea salt
⅓ cup vegetable oil
1 cup alkaline water

Mix coconut flour, coconut flour and salt in a bowl; add the vegetable oil and water, and mix them well until smooth.
Lightly flour a work surface, spread this dough on it, and cut the dough into small squares.
Line the baking sheet with parchment paper, then arrange the dough squares on the baking sheet.
Bake the food at 350°F/175°C for 20 minutes until light golden.
Serve and enjoy.

Per Serving: Calories 371; Fat 18.69g; Sodium 572mg; Carbs 45.08g; Fiber 2.5g; Sugar 2.5g; Protein 6.3g

Za'atar Crackers

Prep time: 10 minutes | **Cook time:** 15 minutes | **Serves:** 3

1⅔ cups generally useful flour
½ teaspoon preparing powder
½ teaspoon salt
1 teaspoon olive oil
½ cup water
1 tablespoon water for brushing the top
1 teaspoon maple syrup
1 tablespoon za'atar flavoring

Preheat the stove to 400°F/200°C.
Add the flour, heating powder, salt, olive oil and water to a large blending bowl; use a huge wooden spoon to blend them until well-combined and smooth (add more flour if the batter is excessively clingy).
On a delicately floured material paper, arrange the batter as thin and even as could reasonably be expected.
Mix 1 tablespoon of water and 1 teaspoon of maple syrup, brush them on the highest point of the batter, and sprinkle the za'atar flavoring on top at that points. Use a pizza shaper length- and widthwise to cut the batter into singular wafers.
Bake them for 15 minutes until they get fresh and brilliant darker.
Let them chill before serving.

Per Serving: Calories 274; Fat 2.19g; Sodium 393mg; Carbs 54.83g; Fiber 1.9g; Sugar 1.74g; Protein 7.32g

Simple Hemp Seed Porridge

Prep time: 5 minutes | **Cook time:** 5 minutes | **Serves:** 6

3 cups cooked hemp seed
1 packet Stevia
1 cup coconut milk

Add the rice and coconut milk to a saucepan, heat them over medium heat for 5 minutes. Make sure to stir constantly.
Turn off the heat, and then mix in the Stevia.
Divide the rice among 6 bowls, and enjoy.

Per Serving: Calories 411; Fat 4.37g; Sodium 25mg; Carbs 82.57g; Fiber 3.6g; Sugar 3.27g; Protein 9.53g

Coconut Cacao Cookies

Prep time: 10 minutes | **Cook time:** 25 minutes | **Serves:** 4

1 cup almond flour
½ cup cacao nibs
½ cup coconut flakes, unsweetened
⅓ cup erythritol
½ cup almond butter
¼ cup nut butter, melted
¼ cup almond milk
Stevia, to taste
¼ teaspoon sea salt

Line the cookie sheet with parchment paper.
Preheat your oven to 350°F/175°C.
Combine all the dry ingredients in a glass bowl.
Add butter, almond milk, vanilla essence, stevia, and almond butter to the bowl, beat them with dry mixture well.
Spoon out of 1 tablespoon of cookie dough on the cookie sheet, and add more dough to make as many as 16 cookies.
Flatten each cookie, bake them for 25 minutes until golden brown.
When cooked, let the cookies sit for 15 minutes before serving.

Per Serving: Calories 474; Fat 33.94g; Sodium 194mg; Carbs 37.22g; Fiber 6.1g; Sugar 23.76g; Protein 10.84g

Coconut Millet Porridge

Prep time: 10 minutes | **Cook time:** 20 minutes | **Serves:** 2

Pinch of sea salt
1 tablespoon coconuts, chopped finely
½ cup unsweetened coconut milk
½ cup millet, rinsed and drained
1½ cups alkaline water
3 drops liquid stevia

Sauté the millet in a non-stick skillet for 3 minutes.
Add salt and water to the skillet, stir well, bring to a boil, and then reduce the heat.
Cook the millet for 15 minutes; stir in the remaining ingredients, and cook for 4 minutes more.
Serve the food with chopped nuts on top.

Per Serving: Calories 332; Fat 16.43g; Sodium 100mg; Carbs 41.09g; Fiber 5.7g; Sugar 3.26g; Protein 6.94g

Spice Spelt Bread

Prep time: 10 minutes | **Cook time:** 20 minutes | **Serves:** 6

2 cups of spelt flour
2 teaspoons of oregano
2 teaspoons of onion powder
¼ teaspoon of cayenne
2 teaspoons of basil
1 tablespoon of pure sea salt
¾ cup of spring water
2 tablespoons of grape seed oil

Mix the spelt flour and all seasonings in a medium bowl; add the grape seed oil and ½ cup of spring water, and continue to mix.
Form the mixture into a dough ball (add more spring water if it is too thick).
Place the dough on a clean work surface, roll out the dough and cover it with flour.
Knead the dough for about 5 minutes until it achieves the desired consistency.
Divide the dough into 6 equal balls; roll out each ball into circles, about 4-inch in diameter.
Heat one flatbread in a non-stick pan over medium heat, flip the flatbread every 2 to 3 minutes until small golden-brown spots appear on both sides.
Do the same with the remaining flatbreads.
Serve warm.

Per Serving: Calories 218; Fat 2.91g; Sodium 7mg; Carbs 42.61g; Fiber 6.9g; Sugar 4.25g; Protein 9.24g

Easy Mango Salsa

Prep time: 15 minutes | **Cook time:** 0 | **Serves:** 6

1 avocado, peeled, pitted and cubed
2 tablespoons fresh key lime juice
1 mango, peeled, pitted and cubed
1 cup cherry tomatoes, quartered
1 tablespoon fresh cilantro, chopped
Sea salt, as required

Mix avocado and lime juice in a large bowl.
Add the remaining ingredients to the bowl, and stir to combine.
Serve and enjoy.

Per Serving: Calories 105; Fat 5.18g; Sodium 29mg; Carbs 15.79g; Fiber 3.7g; Sugar 11.25g; Protein 1.43g

Quick Jackfruit Vegetable Fry

Prep time: 10 minutes | **Cook time:** 15 minutes | **Serves:** 6

2 small onions, finely chopped
2 cups cherry tomatoes, finely chopped
⅛ teaspoon ground turmeric
1 tablespoon olive oil
2 red bell peppers, seeded and chopped
3 cups firm jackfruit, seeded and chopped
⅛ teaspoon cayenne pepper
2 tablespoons fresh basil leaves, chopped
Salt, to taste

Grease the skillet with olive oil.
Sauté onions and bell peppers in a greased skillet for 5 minutes.
Stir in tomatoes and cook for 2 minutes.
Add turmeric, salt, cayenne pepper, and jackfruit., and cook for 8 minutes.
Garnish with basil leaves. Serve warm.

Per Serving: Calories 144; Fat 2.97g; Sodium 36mg; Carbs 30.09g; Fiber 2.8g; Sugar 23.72g; Protein 2.61g

Maple Pistachios Ginger Mix

Prep time: 10 minutes | **Cook time:** 40 minutes | **Serves:** 3-5

2½ cups salted pistachios, shelled
1¼ teaspoons powdered ginger
3 tablespoons pure maple syrup

Combine 1¼ teaspoons powdered ginger and the pistachios to a bowl.
Drizzle the pistachios mixture with 3 tablespoons of maple syrup, and stir well.
Line the baking sheet with parchment paper, and then transfer the mixture to the baking sheet and spread evenly.
Cook the food in the oven at 275°F for about 20 minutes.
When the time is up, take out the baking sheet from oven, stir the food, and cook for further 10 to 15 minutes.
Let the food cool for a few minutes until crispy. Enjoy.

Per Serving: Calories 378; Fat 27.58g; Sodium 265mg; Carbs 25.76g; Fiber 6.1g; Sugar 12.02g; Protein 12.9g

Blueberry-Strawberry Muffins

Prep time: 15 minutes | **Cook time:** 5 hours | **Serves:** 6

¾ cup quinoa flour
¾ cup teff flour
½ teaspoon salt
⅓ cup agave
1 cup fresh coconut milk
¼ cup strawberries, chopped
¼ cup blueberries

Mix the quinoa flour, teff flour, and salt in a bowl.
Combine the agave and coconut milk in another bowl.
Slowly pour the wet ingredients to the dry ingredients, and mix until well-combined. 4. Stir in the berries and mix until well-combined.
Pour the batter in muffin pans, and then place the muffin pans with the batter in the Instant Pot.
Cook the batter on Slow Cook mode for 4 to 5 hours.
Serve warm.

Per Serving: Calories 208; Fat 3.26g; Sodium 216mg; Carbs 37.32g; Fiber 4g; Sugar 5.77g; Protein 7.63g

Squash Onion Hash

Prep time: 5 minutes | **Cook time:** 10 minutes | **Serves:** 2

1 teaspoon onion powder
½ cup onion, finely chopped
2 cups spaghetti squash
½ teaspoon sea salt

Squeeze any extra moisture from spaghetti squash.
Place the squash into a bowl, then add the onion powder, onion, and salt. Stir them to combine.
Spray a non-stick cooking skillet with cooking spray; add the spaghetti squash to the skillet, and cook for 5 minutes over medium heat, untouched.
Flip the hash browns, cook for a few minutes until the desired crispness is reached.
Serve and enjoy.

Per Serving: Calories 47; Fat 0.62g; Sodium 601mg; Carbs 10.61g; Fiber 2.2g; Sugar 4.09g; Protein 1.09g

Jalapeño Zucchini Pancakes

Prep time: 15 minutes | **Cook time:** 8 minutes | **Serves:** 8

12 tablespoons alkaline water
6 large zucchinis, grated
Sea salt, to taste
4 tablespoons ground flax seeds
2 teaspoons olive oil
2 jalapeño peppers, finely chopped
½ cup scallions, finely chopped

Mix water and flax seeds in a bowl.
Heat oil in a large non-stick skillet on medium heat, add zucchini, salt, and black pepper, and sauté for 3 minutes.
Transfer the zucchini to a large bowl, add the scallions, flax seed mixture, and mix thoroughly.
Preheat a griddle, and lightly grease it with cooking spray.
Pour about ¼ of the zucchini mixture into the preheated griddle, and cook for 3 minutes; flip the side carefully, and cook for about 2 more minutes.
Repeat with the remaining mixture in batches. Serve warm.

Per Serving: Calories 35; Fat 2.35g; Sodium 22mg; Carbs 2.78g; Fiber 0.8g; Sugar 0.93g; Protein 1.49g

Lime Avocado Gazpacho

Prep time: 15 minutes | **Cook time:** 0 | **Serves:** 6

3 large avocados, peeled, pitted and chopped
⅓ cup fresh cilantro leaves
3 cups spring water
2 tablespoons fresh key lime juice
¼ teaspoon cayenne powder
Sea salt, as required

Add all the ingredients to the high-speed blender, and pulse them until smooth.
Transfer the mixture into a large bowl.
Cover the bowl and refrigerate to chill for at least 2-3 hours before serving.

Per Serving: Calories 163; Fat 14.76g; Sodium 36mg; Carbs 9.08g; Fiber 6.8g; Sugar 0.76g; Protein 2.06g

Butternut Squash Patties

Prep time: 15 minutes | **Cook time:** 6 minutes | **Serves:** 3

½ cup butternut squash
½ cup diced onion
A dash of sea salt
A dash of cayenne pepper powder
Grapeseed oil

Shred the butternut squash, and place in a bowl.
Add the onion, salt, and cayenne pepper to the bowl, and mix them well.
Form the mixture into small patties.
Heat the grapeseed oil in the sauté pan over medium heat; add the patties, and cook for 3 minutes on all sides.
Serve warm.

Per Serving: Calories 37; Fat 1.57g; Sodium 54mg; Carbs 5.94g; Fiber 1g; Sugar 2.09g; Protein 0.74g

Blueberry Spelt Cakes

Prep time: 15 minutes | **Cook time:** 4 hours | **Serves:** 4

2 cups spelt flour
¼ teaspoon sea salt
¼ cup hemp seeds
1 cup fresh coconut milk
½ cup spring water
2 tablespoons grapeseed oil
½ cup agave
½ cup blueberries

In a bowl, Mix the spelt flour, sea salt, hemp seeds in a bowl; pour in the coconut milk, water, grapeseed oil, and agave, and stir until well-combined.
Add the blueberries to the mixture.
Line the instant pot with parchment paper, and then pour the batter into the pot.
Cook the batter on Slow Cook mode for 4 hours.

Per Serving: Calories 455; Fat 15.48g; Sodium 180mg; Carbs 68.99g; Fiber 10.7g; Sugar 11.18g; Protein 16.57g

Mushroom Pasta with Onion

Prep time: 15 minutes | **Cook time:** 30 minutes | **Serves:** 6

cayenne pepper to taste
3 cups coconut milk
sea salt to taste
3 tablespoons chickpea flour
8 cups mixed mushrooms
1 medium chopped onion
¼ cup avocado oil
1-pound spelt pasta

Pour 8 cups water in to a large pasta pot, add a large handful of sea salt, and spelt pasta. Cook the pasta like the package states. When done, drain.
While the pasta is cooking, heat the avocado oil in a skillet.
Add the onions, mushrooms, and a pinch of salt to the skillet, cook them for 15 minutes until mushrooms have softened and are slightly browned, stirring occasionally (after 5 minutes have passed, turn the heat down; sprinkle the flour over the mushroom mixture and stir well, ensure everything is covered with the flour; let this cook for 1 minutes, and then turn the heat back on).
Add in 1 cup of the coconut milk while constantly stirring and simmer for 1 minutes, break up any clumps that might have formed.
Once the mixture is totally smooth and has thickened a bit, add the rest of the coconut milk.
Add some cayenne to taste, and bring the liquid to a simmer while constantly stirring, resume cooking until the sauce has thickened one more time.
Turn off the heat, and adjust seasonings as needed.
Place the cooked pasta into the sauce, toss well to coat everything.
Divided the food into serving plates, and enjoy.

Per Serving: Calories 460; Fat 15.57g; Sodium 94mg; Carbs 64.16g; Fiber 10.1g; Sugar 15.32g; Protein 19.81g

Conclusion

So, are you ready to shed some weight? The whole body reset is a quick sure way to achieve that. In just 4 weeks, you can gain a healthy lifestyle if you stick to this diet plan and exercise regularly. The whole body reset program is a reminder of what we should be doing to keep our bodies healthy, and a 4-week challenge is just the perfect way to live through that. Pick the right ingredients, make up your mind, bring in some discipline into your eating habits and stay active, and you will be amazed at the health transformation this program has to offer.

Appendix Measurement Conversion Chart

VOLUME EQUIVALENTS (DRY)

US STANDARD	METRIC (APPROXIMATE)
⅛ teaspoon	0.5 mL
¼ teaspoon	1 mL
½ teaspoon	2 mL
¾ teaspoon	4 mL
1 teaspoon	5 mL
1 tablespoon	15 mL
¼ cup	59 mL
½ cup	118 mL
¾ cup	177 mL
1 cup	235 mL
2 cups	475 mL
3 cups	700 mL
4 cups	1 L

VOLUME EQUIVALENTS (LIQUID)

US STANDARD	US STANDARD (OUNCES)	METRIC (APPROXIMATE)
2 tablespoons	1 fl.oz	30 mL
¼ cup	2 fl.oz	60 mL
½ cup	4 fl.oz	120 mL
1 cup	8 fl.oz	240 mL
1½ cup	12 fl.oz	355 mL
2 cups or 1 pint	16 fl.oz	475 mL
4 cups or 1 quart	32 fl.oz	1 L
1 gallon	128 fl.oz	4 L

TEMPERATURES EQUIVALENTS

FAHRENHEIT (F)	CELSIUS (C) (APPROXIMATE)
225°F	107°C
250°F	120°C
275°F	135°C
300°F	150°C
325°F	160°C
350°F	180°C
375°F	190°C
400°F	205°C
425°F	220°C
450°F	235°C
475°F	245°C
500°F	260°C

WEIGHT EQUIVALENTS

US STANDARD	METRIC (APPROXIMATE)
1 ounce	28 g
2 ounces	57 g
5 ounces	142 g
10 ounces	284 g
15 ounces	425 g
16 ounces (1 pound)	455 g
1.5 pounds	680 g
2 pounds	907 g

Made in the USA
Monee, IL
27 January 2023

26403373R00060